A Very Simple Mind
On Tour

Derek Forbes

Published by McNidder & Grace
21 Bridge Street
Carmarthen SA31 3JS
Wales, United Kingdom

www.mcnidderandgrace.com

First published in 2024
©Derek Forbes

All rights reserved. No part of this work may be reproduced or transmitted in any form or by any means, electronic or mechanical, including photocopy, recording, or any information storage or retrieval system, without permission in writing from the publisher.

Derek Forbes has asserted his right to be identified as the author of this work in accordance with the Copyright, Designs and Patents Act 1988.

Every effort has been made to obtain necessary permission with reference to copyright material. The publisher apologises if, inadvertently, any sources remain unacknowledged and will be glad to make the necessary arrangements at the earliest opportunity.

Image credits: cover photo, Virginia Turbett; p.ix, Kimi Gill; p.156, top, Nicole Tammaro; top, p.16 of plate section, Ashley Corr, back flap, Robert Wilson. All other photos courtesy of Derek Forbes.

A catalogue record for this work is available from the British Library.

ISBN 9780857162625 hardback
ISBN 9780857162649 ebook

Designed by JS Typesetting Ltd, Porthcawl
Cover design by Tabitha Palmer

Printed and bound by CPI, Antony Rowe, Wiltshire, UK

For Wendy, my life, my love

Contents

Foreword by Peter Walsh — vii

Intro: Playing a Good Riff — xi

1. The Best Year Ever … — 1
2. When Harry Met Betty — 23
3. Young Derek — 27
4. Better Guitars and Gigs — 35
5. Simple Minds — 43
    First Rehearsal — 43
    First Gig The Mars Bar — 44
    Zoom Records — 47
    First Album Flight *Life in a Day* — 49
    On Tour — 52
    Magazine, the *Secondhand Daylight* Tour — 54
    Back on Tour Again – and it's still 1979 — 57
    Real to Real Cacophony — 61
    Real to Real Cacophony Tour — 65
    Old Grey Whistle Test New York — 68
    Home Turf Again: University Tour — 70
    Bigger Things to Come — 74
    Empires and Dance — 75
    Peter Gabriel Tour — 78
    Kelly Marie and the Disposable Camera — 82
    Signed by Virgin — 83
    'Glittering Prize' and *New Gold Dream* — 90
    Steadying the Ship — 99
    New Gold Dream Tour — 100
    Time Out and Then Back Again — 104
    'Waterfront' — 116

6. Once More into the Breeks	119
7. Simple Minds, Take Two	131
Back with Simple Minds	133
Back on Tour	135
The Last-Ever Gig	141
8. What Next?	143
Outro: Throwing the Last Stone	147
Outtakes	149
On Tour with the Crew	150
In the Van	152
A Typical Tour Day	153
My Guitars	155
Other Bands I have played in	155
Not Forgetting	158
Words From …	159
Acknowledgements	164

Foreword

My early musical influences came from a wide variety of genres and artists. On the one side there was R&B: Stevie Wonder, George Benson, Johnson Brothers, Quincy Jones. On the other side alternative art rock: Talking Heads, David Bowie, Roxy Music, Peter Gabriel. When I first heard Simple Minds, it was like listening to a hybrid of all the bands I loved. One of the things I liked most was how the drums and bass worked together: beneath the distinctive interplay between guitar and keyboards there was a powerful engine with a deep, punchy bass line driving the music forward. Enter Derek Forbes!

The first time I saw Derek perform was in Liège, during the Simple Minds' *Sons and Fascination* tour. Songs like 'In Trance as Mission', 'Celebrate' and 'Love Song' struck me particularly. The way he moved on stage, it was as if he was connected to a different source – coming from somewhere deep inside, through his whole body and not just his hands. Much later I saw him playing with Propaganda in Munich and it was the same thing: hypnotic, mesmerising, as if he was in a world of his own.

In the world of bass playing there were many different styles and techniques emerging at the time. Whether playing pick or finger style, slap bass or on a fretless, Derek was master of them all. 'Colours Fly' and 'Big Sleep' worked well playing in a slap bass style, but Derek had his own technique of hammering down but not plucking up, so it didn't sound too funky. It was more percussive, more primal. Although he was a very physical player, he was undoubtedly one of the more relaxed musicians I've worked with in the studio over the years. He never seemed to feel the pressure, or if he did, he never showed it.

Laying down the rhythm tracks for 'New Gold Dream', we wanted to get bass, drums and at least one basic guitar track down at the same time. I didn't want to risk losing the energy and feel of the live performance by doing too many overdubs afterwards, so it was important to get as much as possible in one take. Derek had the stamina and skill to do repeated takes, each one as good as the other, and the focus to keep it sounding fresh every time. These were pretty tricky bass parts, but as always, he made it look easy. He was also willing to try the different approaches and ideas I had in some of the more atmospheric songs like 'King is White' and 'Somebody Up There Likes You', where in the interests of precision and sound quality we simplified the recording by adding a few overdubs. He would of course have been technically capable of playing it all at the same time perfectly but was cool enough not to need to prove it.

Many of Derek's bass parts were based on circular phrases, a 2- or 4-bar cycle which repeated throughout the song. In a way they worked more like guitar riffs than traditional bass lines, which focus more on playing the root notes of the chords. The beauty of this is that the music changes above it while the bass stays the same. It's one of the reasons that the album *New Gold Dream* sounded so special, and this was a core characteristic of the Simple Minds sound. Some of the *New Gold Dream* songs required a funkier touch on the drums, which is where my old mate Mel Gaynor came into the picture – and that collaboration between Mel and Derek led to a great pairing.

Derek was always fun to be with, both in and out of the studio, and we had many special moments where he had me falling about in fits of laughter. I remember making home videos with him up in Fife during the rehearsals for *New Gold Dream*, where like kids we filmed paper planes flying over the loch to simulate Lancaster Bombers, accompanied by the *Dambusters* theme tune. It was moments like this when Derek's love of the ridiculous, and his ability to find the simple joy in things, shone through.

Moving down to London for the recording there were late nights at the Columbia hotel in Bayswater, raiding the kitchen and consuming vast quantities of Marmite sandwiches to cure the munchies, and keeping the bar open till the early hours. I think it was on one of these late nights that Charlie and he came up with a nickname for me – Arthur of the Britons.

When we were working at Manor Studios in Oxford, I remember him calling me on the studio phone one afternoon to ask me to join him in the games room for a frame of snooker. It seemed strangely urgent, so I went over to the house with some trepidation, thinking there might be a practical joke about to happen. Walking into the room I saw that the table was set, all balls positioned correctly with one exception. Where the red balls were usually located sat a rather large hedgehog! The

Foreword

poor animal was returned to the garden without delay after the joke had passed.

Many years later, during the recording of *Néapolis*, Derek would pick me up from Glasgow airport each week in a bright red Audi Quattro. Jim and Charlie had purchased this vehicle expressly for the two of us to commute the 70 miles to and from the studio in Loch Earn. It was always a hilarious journey, during which we'd talk about family, music, and our love of British comedy – *Monty Python*, *Fawlty Towers*, *Derek and Clive*. He knew all their sketches by heart. He was, in a way, the comedian of the band, a bit of a clown, always up for a laugh. He had what I would call a kind of *Carry On* sense of humour (probably derived from watching too many *Carry On* films!) and he also did a wicked impersonation of an old man, harumphing around the studio.

What about lasting impressions, legacy? One of the most rewarding things that can happen when you're a music producer is to know that people appreciate the music you are creating. Over the 40 years since I recorded with Derek, there have been countless occasions when I have been asked what it was like to work with him back then: *How did you get that sound? What kind of a person is he?* Looking back, it was a moment in time which shaped both of our lives massively, and I'm proud and grateful to have had the opportunity to be part of the big story and to have made the best of it, for all of us.

Peter Walsh, September 2023

Peter Walsh, Holy Mountain Studios, London

Intro: Playing a Good Riff

On 22 June 1956, I came into this world and battled with double pneumonia and later a double hernia, everything happening in stereo. This book tells the tale of my journey into music and of the early days of Simple Minds, where five young men took on the world. It was 1977. Playing bass was almost alien to me, a 20-year-old Derek Forbes, who'd been a lead guitar player since 1971. I had been asked to join Simple Minds permanently, but still couldn't break the 'chord' that joined me and my guitar in favour of the bass. However, my beloved Gibson Les Paul guitar, my pride and joy, was stolen from a rehearsal room in Glasgow. After that, I decided to say yes to Simple Minds and become their bass guitarist. In time I went on to be voted the best bass player in Scotland and recognised around the world. There are tales that will make you spit your tea down through your nose in uncontrollable laughter, tales that may shock, and tales that will warm your heart. I share with you stories from travels on the road, dabbles with mind-bending substances, unfortunate accidents in the trouser regions as well as glamorous meetings with superstars. We laughed together, we laughed at each other, we had fights and arguments, we learned to work with luminaries of the music industry, but most of all, we always had fun. This is my truth. All verbatim, all kosher, no horse shit! A most splendid read, I hope. And if I have fucked up any of the stories, dates or names, then let me know.

1. The Best Year Ever ...

This year was going to be an incredible year for Simple Minds. We were heading on tour to Australia and New Zealand again. *Sparkle in the Rain* had just been released and it had gone straight to Number One in the UK. We were headlining, with the Eurythmics supporting us, and Talking Heads preceding us, and they would play with the Pretenders supporting them. It was incredibly exciting for the band. We left the UK in January 1984 on a British Airways flight, first class all the way.

When we got to Sydney, we were welcomed by screaming fans. At the hotel, the Southern Cross, we met up with all the other bands, complete with their children and including some very young babies. It was like Supertramp on tour, with buggies and nappies and Breakfast in Australia. There were lots of rock luminaries milling about and chatting. Packs of promoters and their teams there, and an army of record company representatives too. I met Lisa Gaye Watt, and we got on like a house on fire. Dave Stewart teamed up with us as we breathed in Australia together. We had a TV show later that week to do for 'Molly' Meldrum at his home in Melbourne.

Good old Melbourne, birthplace of my lovely wife to be. We had our first gig on 27 January 1984 at the Narara Festival. Jim spoke of it being a disaster, but I have no recollection of that at all. I really enjoyed it. 'Waterfront' was doing well in the Antipodes, which was great. During these days we had a barbecue laid on by our record company pals. It was at Palm Beach just North of Sydney, where *Home and Away* was shot. It was a proper Aussie barbie, and we got pissed and danced about the beach like a bunch of eejits. Soon we were off to the next shows in Melbourne. I had become friendly with the Talking Heads band, so Lisa, Dave Stewart and myself partied with them every night until we left for New Zealand. One night in Melbourne I was standing with David Byrne. We were looking out of the window at the swimming pool below. Someone had ordered loads of pizzas, so David and I started skimming the boxes over the water of the pool. We must have thrown a good load of them. Suddenly David turned to me and said, 'Hey, you're from

Scotland.' I said, 'Well spotted, that man!' He then went on to tell me he was Scottish, and that he came from Dumbarton, and I reminded him that this was the third or fourth time he had told me that.

Next stop, Auckland, New Zealand. By this time 'Waterfront' had gone to Number One in the charts. We were playing on the North Island, totally different to the South Island. The gig was at the Sweetwaters Festival, and what a gig it was! Limos were available to take the artists anywhere they chose and at any time of the day. At the gig I could see, in the front rows, hordes of crazy-looking bikers, including Māori bikers. They did look the business. The stage was at the bottom of a steep hill. At the top of the hill was a lake. There were helicopters taking people for rides over the audience of tens of thousands of people. At one point a helicopter lost control and had to ditch in the lake. Flares were going off everywhere, and each side of the audience became at war with each other. One side threw cans and bottles in their hundreds at the other half, the other threw everything back. It was like a scene out of *Apocalypse Now*. One man decided to push his way through the crowd to the front of stage. He had a bottle of kerosene, took a gulp, lit it, and burned his way through the people. Some people's hair was set alight. Soon the guy was battered to the ground and taken away. Another person tried to drive a Transit van into the crowd. It was overturned, the driver was pulled out and then kicked out of the festival. Though it was chaotic in the crowd our performance was still great. The gig was great, and we appeared to go down well – as did the Eurythmics. At the beginning I watched Annie Lennox warming and vibing up before striding onstage looking full of confidence. She really did take this showbiz lark seriously! A wonderfully talented artist and lady.

Time to head back to Australia for a final fling and a cheerio to all of our new friends. We arrived in Sydney and after a day or so we travelled to Canberra. I tried the new fad that was happening in Australia, Tequila Slammers. I was out of my gourd when I finally left the club. The last show was on 9 February at Selina's, the incredible hotel and nightclub where I met Robert Plant of Led Zeppelin and where he asked me if I wanted to go to Elton John's stag night in Manly Vale. We laughed at this one! We left beautiful Australia a few days later for Ireland.

Our first gig in Ireland was in Galway's Leisurelands Centre. This was the first time we had played in Galway, and the audience were fantastic. Next day we were at the City Hall in Cork. This is the home of Murphy's

Stout, Cork's answer to Guinness. Charlie, Mick and I went out to test it. On 20 February we went back to Dublin to play Gallagher's Hall. OK it's not called that, but it is St Francis Xavier's Hall – funnily, the sound man, who was no saint, had the very same name! After the sound check and before the gig Charlie, Mick, Mel and me went out for a drink and ordered Asti Spumante – this became a habit thereafter.

We had loads of great times in Dublin, especially in the bars, restaurants, and later Lillie's Bordello in the '90s. On 21 February we did our second night at SFX, which never disappointed. The next day we were back over the border in Belfast. Due to a very high demand for tickets, we were to play two gigs on the same evening at the Ulster Hall in Belfast. There had been queues of fans all around the Hall and streets, waiting to get in for the show. It was a very cold day, and people braved the freezing conditions. The first set started at half past six. I remember a scarf being thrown onstage and it landed on my bass guitar; I just took it off and booted it back into the audience. At half past nine we came onstage and did the show all over again. That night we got – or should I say, *I* got – totally pissed. In the morning we had a travel day. I was still steaming drunk as we left to board the small plane taking us to Edinburgh. It had no toilet, so I was in a cold sweat the whole way over the Irish sea. I managed to keep my clothes in perfect order, thank you.

We had two shows at the Edinburgh Playhouse, on 24–25 February. It's a great theatre, and both nights were fantastic. Although we are from Glasgow, Edinburgh is our second home, we love the place. On the 26th we played The Caird Hall in Dundee. There was a real buzz in the Hall, the audience cheered us on after every song. February 27, we go to the home of Clan Forbes, Aberdeen. We played at The Capitol Theatre. About halfway through the gig, a girl jumped up onto the stage and put her arms around me. I was surprised. Was it my aftershave?

On 28–29 February and 1–2 March we played Barrowland. Four in a row. We stayed at the Beacons Hotel in the Park area of Glasgow, diagonally across from where I sit and write these lines. I live in the area now, and I often see hordes of students walking past my house. They mostly stay at the hotel which is a youth hostel now. It's now hard to believe: I can still see Mel Gaynor ripping off the door of Lenny Love's room demanding his per diems.

The Barrowland gigs were incredible. Absolutely packed every night. The horsehair-sprung floor was jumping and we could see the definite sway of the fans from the stage. There were girls fainting at the front throughout the shows. One was mouthing something naughty at me, and then she pretended to faint. She got carried over the stage, as that was the only space the St John Ambulance workers had to work with. They passed me with the girl in the stretcher, and she looked up and winked at me from the stretcher.

On March 3 we played one of the most revered gigs of my tenure with the band, Newcastle's very own City Hall. The *New Gold Dream* tour had been sensational in the past, and now, it was the turn *of Sparkle in the Rain*. The show was everything we expected and more. Brilliant gig with the sons and daughters of the River Tyne, brilliant people.

We arrive next in Liverpool at the Empire Theatre. This has an enormous stage, so I had to do a bit more walking around to make sure I played to everyone. Keeps you fit, this rock lark. My Beatles fix complete, we headed off to Nottingham for the next gig. I have played gigs here with Simple Minds, Spear of Destiny with my great mate Kirk Brandon, Big Country, the Alarm, Los Mondo Bongo, Propaganda and my own band Derek Forbes and the Dark. I am making myself thirsty, longing for a session at Ye Olde Tripp to Jerusalem, the pub next to Nottingham Castle, where Richard the Lionheart congregated before setting off on their Crusade.

On 6 March we head to the Apollo in Manchester. Another wonderful place and gig. I still remember supporting Magazine there, listening to them playing 'The Light Pours out of Me' and watching wee John McGeoch shredding those parts. There was nobody like him, RIP.

We headed next to the scene of the crime, Leeds University, scene of the Who's *Live at Leeds* (as you know by now, one of my favourite albums). Not only were we treading the boards of our heroes, we were also using their equipment, hired from their headquarters in Shepperton Studios. Do you remember Jim Kerr using a golden Shure SM58 microphone? It was Roger Daltrey's! Kenny Hyslop had used Keith Moon's drum riser on one of the tours. We had a lot of the Who's crew and some crew from Pink Floyd. The best of the best!

I was in my element playing there. One thing was for sure, I got 'famous value while shopping'. I bought a Gibson Les Paul 'Black Beauty' for £650 on tour with Kirk Brandon's 10:51. Thank you, Leeds, you have always been wonderful.

By the time we were at the Odeon in Birmingham, Jim and I were both suffering with a very high temperature. I stood and played, hardly able to stand, but soldiered on until Jim's voice completely went, and we had to cut the show short. The next gigs were cancelled and rebooked for later. We needed some time off to recover.

A European tour was now being arranged, starting on the 24th of March in Scandinavia. We went to play the Isstadion in Stockholm, Sweden. Jim and I had fully recovered from our terrible bout of flu and were looking forward to treading the boards again. I remember one of the guys from our agency, Frontier Booking International (FBI), in New York had come to the gig to see us. His name was John Huey. Our show was really well received, and John took me to the side for one helluva compliment: I was, he said, more of a Black player than any other white player he had seen, such was the soul in my playing.

Back in the dressing room we had a special guest in Thomas Johansson, management partner to Stig Anderson for ABBA. Thomas asked me if I could write some songs for the girls, now that ABBA had stopped playing. I said if I had time, I would give it a try, but my time was all about Simple Minds, and I never had a chance to work on anything else. I was asked to play on Frida's album with Phil Collins, Mark Brzezicki (of Big Country), my great friend Kirsty MacColl and others, but again I was cup tied, and couldn't make it.

Then to Denmark, down to Germany and over to Belgium. We approach Brussels and book into the Hotel Métropole. On the day of the gig, Mel, Mick, Charlie and I had breakfast outside at the tables set up just in front of the hotel. Those were great times and I really miss them. Two nights in Brussels playing to our fabulous Belgian fans, and we move to Brielsport, in Deinze. Then we go to one of the best arena venues in Holland, the Ahoy Sportpalies on 31 March and 1 April. I remember walking in to find a strange woman accompanied by one of the crew. A well-dressed lady, grasping a big leather bag. She was a drug dealer, coming in to supply us and others with whatever we required. At the time this was normal in the industry for hard-working travelling bands – it was accepted that you may need something to keep you going or calm you down on these grueling tours. The Ahoy gigs were magnificent. What a place to play. It was enormous and packed with adoring Simple Minds fans who swayed and danced along to the music. We felt like we had arrived. If we had wondered before, this blew our doubts out of the water.

The next day we played our old favourite, the Stadthalle Offenbach. We were delighted to be back. After the gig, it was off to bed and up early for the drive to Hamburg, one time home of the Beatles. We played the Markthalle once again, a favourite venue of the band. We did have a wee wander around the red-light district, namely the Reeperbahn.

The gig at the Markthalle was, guess what, fantastic. It looks like a building where cattle auctions are held, but '*geil*' (cool) all the same. If you ever visit Hamburg then go into the Hauptbahnhof, or train station; it's well worth a visit, for shops, food, books, trains, and journeys on to faraway places. On 6 April we go to my soon-to-be haunting ground, Düsseldorf. We played the Phillipshalle, and felt that this was another landmark for us on our journey upwards; the young German audience were superb.

On 7 April we detoured into France for a gig. On the next day, we arrive in Munich to play the Circus Krone, which I had seen many a time in old WWII footage. This is where rallies were held by Madalf Heatlump and the Nasties, as John Lennon wrote in *In His Own Write*. It was an awesome place and, like it says, a circus, under a huge tent. A where young Oskar would have been in his element; if you have read or seen *The Tin Drum*, you will know who I mean. I love Munich, it is such a colourful place – and a visit to the House of 1000 Beers is well worth it.

Next stop Italy. A day off on our way to Mestre, Venice. How lucky are we to get to play in these wonderful, iconic places, full of history. We got here quick enough to arrange dinner in the balmy Italian evening. We boarded one of the beautiful wooden water taxis, and sailed to a restaurant on the bank of one of the tiny canals. It was very warm for this time of year, and the canal water had an unforgiving pong. The food at the restaurant was lovely and there were around nine or ten courses. I had to go for a sleep between courses and then returned and just carried on – as the saying goes, 'Don't eat till you're full, eat till you're tired.'

As usual the Italians were so passionate about the band, and we left Venice with a big collective cheesy grin on our faces. The next day we headed to Reggio-Emilia, where the fans were getting ever wilder. We arrived at the venue, which had a huge fence right around the building, and there were a lot of fans waiting impatiently, pressing up against the gates and fences. Safely through the gates, we then sat in the dressing room for some snacks and drinks. Time for a bit of shut-eye for some of us, as the partying every night was taking its toll. The venue was another of the big sports halls. It was a magic gig as usual, and after the show, we met fans and dignitaries before boarding the minibus. As we got to the gates, there was complete mayhem. There was a sea of fans crowding us, climbing onto the minibus, and peering in the windows. We eventually made a dash for it. What a great experience though, but I wouldn't like it to be like that every day.

The next gig is the Teatro Tenda in the Lampugnano area of Milan. This is, as you can probably work out, another theatre tent, with an official capacity of 7,000. When we stepped onstage that night there were 14,000 people: the crowd were fighting and pushing and shouting and certainly full of passion. We were amazed by this incredible reception, and the gig was astounding. Thanks to the Gods that we were not the support act that night! I will never forget that feeling. We were home and dry in Italy, that was for sure.

In the morning of 13 April, we made our way to Zürich in Switzerland. The Volkshaus was the next gig that night. I love Austria. We went onstage and we were greeted by our lovely audience. The set was 'East at Easter', 'Up On the Catwalk', 'Book of Brilliant Things', 'Glittering Prize', 'The American', 'King is White and in the Crowd', 'Speed Your Love to Me', 'Someone, Somewhere in Summertime', 'Promised You a Miracle', 'Big Sleep' and 'Waterfront'. During 'King is White and in the Crowd', Jim suddenly jumped up in the air and sang, 'I've got a luvverly bunch of coconuts'. I was choking, laughing; what just happened? Was he going mad, was he tripping? No! He was in love. At that time, he was besotted by his new girlfriend Chrissie Hynde, and he just took a maddy onstage that night. I am convinced there will be a recording of that moment somewhere.

Then we're into the French-speaking area of Switzerland, and Lausanne. Next stop the Théâtre de Verdure, in Nice, France. I recollect doing the gig here, and I have memories of promenading on the front in the intense heat, under stunning azure, cloudless skies. I also have flashbacks to the beautiful hotel on the front, where we stayed that night. On 16 April we are in Toulouse, at the Halle aux Grains. Same deal, wonderful place, incredible French people taking the time to come and see us. The next day we drove past endless vineyards. Marseille was next; it seemed almost like a pirate town and there were certainly a few dodgy characters down by the harbour. The gig was full and buzzing.

Next we drove down in the tour bus overnight to Madrid, to play two nights at Morasol. Great gig: Mel was up at the front conducting the crowd with a drumstick. He really is a huge character. I felt I was home! My love affair with España has never faltered. I managed to speak in Spanish to the crowd a few times – that went down well. One phrase that really went down really well was '*Dame tus manos*', which translates to '*Give me your hands*' – the arena was a sea of hands.

On 20 April we are at the Pacha Auditorium in Valencia. This is an upstairs venue, so quite a challenging get-in, but the show was really worth the struggle. ('Tangent alert' – a year later I would be there with the band Propaganda. It was the night when smoking cannabis was legalised in Spain – or, at least, Valencia. Propaganda had a meal the night before our gig, and we sparked up a few joints in the restaurant after our meal.) After the show we got in our bunks on the tour bus, ending up in Barcelona the next morning.

Next stop, we played the Palais d'Hiver in Lyon. Lyon was always a great town for us to play; the people there are so friendly. I remember that one of our mad fans, who travelled to lots of gigs with us, was dancing to every song we did at the soundcheck. She was a special little lady, and a top fan. Another top night and away we go to another great French town, Rennes. Then Le Zenith in Paris. According to online reports, this was Simple Minds' finest hour – we played out of our skins to the crazy Parisian fans. What a great end to our European jaunt. I would dearly love to move to France, but don't tell my publisher that.

Charlie Burchill, Mel Gaynor and Derek, Paris

We headed back to good old Blighty, booking into the Columbia hotel. As usual our return to Bayswater Road saw us bump into a plethora of musical stars of the time. ABC, Depeche Mode, George Michael, and many more. I remember one time we were staying at the Columbia hotel and were due to meet the actor Peter Firth, courtesy of the lovely Frankie, who had looked after us so well at the farm in Scotland where we wrote the album *New Gold Dream*. So, we were all sitting together on a big sofa in the lounge of the Columbia Hotel. The door opened, and we saw Frankie and Peter coming towards us. We loved the film *Tess*, and the connection to Nastassja Kinski, so we were buzzing, and a bit in awe. As he approached, he gave off an air of coolness, and we got up to greet him. We shook hands and sat back down on the sofa. There was a big armchair for Peter right in front of us. He sat down, as cool as you like, but was a bit too forceful on the armchair, and next thing, the chair had toppled backwards with him in it. We burst out laughing hysterically, and Peter's face was scarlet. What an icebreaker! We all got on famously, and shared Earl Grey tea and cucumber sandwiches.

Our next gig was meant to be at the Birmingham Odeon on the 5 May 1984. However, the gig was cancelled due to Jim's wedding to Chrissie Hynde in New York. While Jim was jetting off to NY the rest of the band had a little sabbatical around London, which helped us to refresh no end. We rehearsed, had photographs taken, did a video, went to see a flim, did a bit more shopping with Charlie – whatever we did, we did it together. We had a good run of UK gigs coming up before we were USA-bound, so we had to get over to Grosvenor Square, to the American Embassy, to sort out work visas.

7 May, we went to Leeds University and played a blinder. On 9 May we headed down south to Cornwall for a gig at the Cornwall Coliseum, St Austell. This is where our new make-up and wardrobe guy, Peter Kozub, gave me a haircut before I went onstage. He cut me twice with the samurai scissors he was using, and I asked if the hair creation he had left me with was a bowl cut. I left the dressing room for the stage and popped back to retrieve my guitar plectrum to find he was lying flat out on a chair, out of his face on some substance or other. What a man!

Later that month, we started an eight-night run in London, at Hammersmith Odeon. We stayed in a hotel in Piccadilly, across the road from The Ritz. The first night was an amazing experience, the second the same, on the third the gloss was beginning to erode, and by the time we got to the last night, we were thoroughly bored. Don't get me wrong, it was an honour to play that many times at such a prestigious venue. How actors keep their sanity intact on theatre runs is way beyond my comprehension. All said and done, the number of people who came to see us was tremendous, and we still applaud you all for being there: 35,200 people! Had Simple Minds finally landed?

Next it was our turn to jet off to New York! We landed in NY early to allow us all time to get used to the new time zone. Mick, Charlie and I went out shopping to the Rolex shop in Manhattan and bought Chrissie and Jim matching watches as our wedding present to them.

During the evening of the 26 May we played at Ritchie Coliseum, College Park. It was raining heavily at this gig and during the show a skylight broke above us, and water poured out, hitting my amp. I thought, *Fuck this, as soon as I touch my microphone I will fry*, so I stopped singing anywhere near the mic. I remember that Jim wasn't too happy! We played the Up All Night Ballroom in Irvington, New Jersey on 27 May. This was memorable because some drunken twat grabbed a drum microphone and started singing 'It's a grand old team to play for' which we could hear through the monitors. I wanted to boot his arse, but we all laughed at the cheek of the zoomer. 29 May next gig Orpheum Theatre, Boston, Massachusetts – our fourth year playing Boston. It was good to meet an old friend here, a Japanese photographer, who had been at the original Simple Minds gigs in the early days.

We head north, through the border into Canada and arrive in Montreal. From there we made our way to Toronto, Ontario, for four nights at Massey Hall. This venue just shows how big the band had become, with residencies everywhere, worldwide. Toronto for four days!

On 7 June we did an overnighter to Ann Arbor, Michigan – a beautiful little place, and a fine gig. Then Chicago, Illinois. Another good show, and we head up northwest to Canada again. This time it is the Queen Elizabeth Hall in Vancouver. My girlfriend at the time had met up with me now and joined me on the tour, a huge mistake on my part. We were in our bunk as we reached the border. The border police came onboard and asked for our passports, so we handed the passports through the curtain, and peeped out to show our faces.

Our popularity meant that we were booked to play the Hollywood Palladium again on 17 June. A couple of people in the audience from the front of the stage shouted at me to do a solo. I threw in a couple of slaps and pop but didn't veer from my task in hand. They cheered their heads off. American audiences are right up there with the best, though nothing beats my hometown Glasgow crowd.

Bill Graham, our US manager, had booked us into the Warfield Theatre in San Francisco. This was the penultimate gig, and it was amazing. The last gig on the 19 June was at Perkins Palace, Pasadena, and I then headed to New York. There I partied hard with the Psychedelic Furs. I was trying to pin down when I would have free time to go into the studio with them but, as usual, free time was a commodity that was very scarce in the Simple Minds world.

Our next stop was Germany, via Holland, for our famous show at the Westfalenhalle in Dortmund. The gig was on 24 June, and it turned out to be one of the most loved gigs of many a Simple Minds fan.

I had lots of wines and lines before getting on my flight back, and I collapsed into my hotel in Holland for my overnight stay, before crossing the border in the morning to Germany. The band were already there, and we met up to share stories of our five days off. I drank black coffee, which went through me like a Porsche. By the time we got to the gig I was fine, though.

I had been messing about with the start of 'The American'. The audience were going crazy by the time we got on stage. How had we managed, as a band, to come so far? We were like the Prodigal Sons coming home, or in my case the Protestant son. The reception couldn't have been better. We started with 'East at Easter', then straight into the raucous jungle drums of 'Up on the Catwalk', followed by the incredible 'Book of Brilliant Things'. The audience swayed along with us and sang every word. They were ecstatic by this time. We carried on with 'Glittering Prize', to the delight of all, and then the *pièce de résistance,* my reworked version of 'The American' I started on my own with a sort of cowboy theme which became known as the *Bonanza* version. We had the fans in a frenzy.

Jim sang a new part just for that occasion, where he named lots of American cities that meant a lot to us and especially Jim as he was now Chrissie Hynde's husband. Philadelphia, Akron, New York City ... and then the whole band burst into life and the old familiar song was ignited and people were dancing, singing and fainting from the sheer might of Simple Minds in full flight. This was a truly special moment. We got a bit mysterious with the next song 'King is White and in the Crowd', which is one of my favourite compositions. We exploded into 'Speed Your Love to Me', and cooled down for the ethereal strains of 'Someone Somewhere in Summertime'. Up we went again to another favourite which Kenny Hyslop had a big hand in, 'Promised You a Miracle'. And now we unleash 'Big Sleep' to calm everyone down, which acts as a welcome break from the thunderous cacophony that we have, till now, presented to the incredible throng of happy people. The silence is broken by a single note, played over and over, and the fireworks are fizzing in anticipation, waiting for the whole band to start. Bang, bang, it's time for 'Waterfront', and the sweat was lashing all around, including us, and the run to the end of the show had begun. 'New Gold Dream' starts, and the people's joy can be felt in the air. We did an amazing job, especially with the voice and answer part, Jim and I belting out 'Take Me to the River', an old favourite routine that always delights the crowd, and now it's time for 'Love Song'. This gig goes down as one of the finest gigs Simple Minds had ever done, and we, the band, were ecstatic.

The next gig on the Simple Minds tour was Schüttorf again, at Vechteweise, another festival, on 30 June. The following gigs were headline shows at Torhout and Werchter on 7 and 8 July respectively. We were headlining both nights, and below us were Lou Reed, Joe Jackson, Paul Young, David Johansen, Nona Hendryx, Chris Rea, and The Alarm. Both shows were magnificent, and we were becoming popular regulars in these Belgian towns.

It was now time to get back home and prepare for the massive tour supporting the Pretenders in the USA. The first gig was on 25 July – and yes, it's still 1984! The big day came for gig number one. Toronto was, and still is, one of our biggest strongholds in Canada. It was a beautiful sunny day when we made our way to Kingswood Music Theatre. That day we were in the dressing room early, and things were getting exciting and a bit boisterous with Mel Gaynor and me. We started dummy fighting which resulted in me booting him in the arse, and unfortunately resulted in me breaking my big toe. What a start to a huge tour! Luckily, I was a veteran of broken metatarsals, and just hopped around the stages until it was completely healed. We had a great reception, and this was only a warm-up gig! Our pairing with The Treebenders, as we called them, was going to be a successful one. Afterwards, we went back to our hotel, the Four Seasons, and sat with members of the Pretenders, and John McEnroe, of all people! What a lovely guy, and not at all like the image that had preceded him in his tennis days.

Mel Gaynor on the bus on tour with Simple Minds, USA, 1984

On 27 July we moved into the good old USA, to Portland, Maine on the East Coast where we performed at the Civic Centre. The Pretenders played their hearts out, and Chrissie Hynde certainly owned that stage. It was such a fun time, with Robbie McIntosh, Rupert Black and our very own pal Malcolm Foster. Jim was away with Chrissie and the Pretenders drummer Martin Chambers. Martin was a big character. If he met you and wanted to be your friend, he would challenge you to a fight, to bond with you at the fight's end. We became friends – without a blow, may I add.

One of our gigs for us was in Cuyahoga Falls in Ohio. I remember that we stayed in Akron, as it wasn't too far away from the Falls. This was a home gig for Chrissie Hynde, and there was a sense of pride flowing through the audience that night. We drove overnight and woke up in Saratoga Springs with a day off. It was now 31 July, and the sun was still shining. We had breakfast at the hotel, and I saw Jack Hues of Wang Chung run by in an attempt at keeping fit.

This was a day off, and we found out that the Cars were playing at the same place where we were performing the following night. We had a confab and decided that we should all go to the gig. I think it was our wardrobe person, Tessie Chua, who suggested that we hire mopeds. And there we were, about ten of us, on mopeds, making our way to the show. It was a huge gig. There was a tree-lined road leading up to the backstage area. We rode in and, to our horror, we saw rows and rows of Harley Davidson bikes with the biker gang attached to them, staring at us! One cool guy said: 'Burn rubber, man', and the majority of them sneered and laughed. We drove by, thoroughly embarrassed. The gig was incredible, though. Ric Ocasek was amazing on guitar and Benjamin Orr was a star.

A welcome day off followed and we were off for a day out with Ian Copland, the CEO from our agency, FBI. We went to his house in the Hampton for boating, fishing and shooting. Later we had dinner, which was cooked by the wonderful actress Courtney Cox, Ian's girlfriend at that time. She was lovely and had a real Scarlett O'Hara Southern twang to her voice: 'D'y'all like squash?' After a fun day of boating and shooting cans, we travelled back to New York to our hotel, where I met up with Graham Nash, as I had done many times before, usually at the hotel bar.

Derek relaxing with a wee drink on tour with Simple Minds, New York

The Best Year Ever ...

Courtney Cox, Mel Gaynor at Madison Square Gardens

On 7 August was the most memorable gig of that tour: Madison Square Gardens in New York. We travelled back to New York overnight, still quite pissed, but managed to get up bright and early and get ourselves back into our New York Hotel. Once surfaced and after a snack, a man came up to me. He was with John Lydon (Johnny Rotten). The man showed me a photo of himself and John. He asked me what was wrong with the photograph, and I said, 'You're in it!' John rolled about laughing. I got on really well with John. Old punks never die!

We arrive at Madison Square Gardens and do our soundcheck. It was nearly showtime, and I was talking to Courtney Cox in the dressing room. We got the call to go, and on we trooped. The band were initially a bit disappointed by an audience who were arriving in dribs and drabs. I told the band we should play like the place was full, and that the people who had paid for their ticket and turned up deserved the best we could give. We did just that, and about a third of the way into the gig the place was full. We stayed to watch Chrissie, Malcolm, Robbie, Rupert and Martin. They were excellent. Back at our hotel Charlie, Mick and I sat in the hotel lobby with some fans. My pal Adam Clayton from U2 joined us, and Stephen Stills sat with us too. The hotel manager was trying to throw out some of the fans and was a bit rude. Stephen Stills suddenly jumped up on his feet and roasted the manager. The guy crumbled and the fans stayed on. Good man.

At Providence, Rhode Island on 9 August, nothing much happened. But it did remind me of a scene in *Spinal Tap*. A guy sitting in the front seats looked bored and gave the band the thumbs down. I am sure he was a bit of a hippy and found our groovy sounds a bit too alien for him. Oh well, each to his own.

After gigs at Allentown, and Worcester, Massachusetts we were onto Toronto for another well-earned day off. We booked into the Four Seasons and after breakfast went for a walk. We got back to the hotel at lunchtime and sat outside with Chrissie and John McEnroe again. I introduced myself, again, to John, but he said: 'I know who you are', which was nice! Next day we played somewhere in Toronto, but nobody seems to know where; good drugs!

I do know that we did two nights in Clarkston, Georgia, then San Diego on 16 August. I love San Diego. I have played the Belly-Up Tavern there a few times since my Simple Minds days, and I have also played the Belly-Up Tavern in Aspen, Colorado, where I met the now sadly departed Taylor Hawkins of the Foo Fighters, who was a great friend and fan of Big Country drummer Mark Brzezicki.

After San Diego, we had to head back east to Chicago, Illinois. I remember rolling about on the floor with Paul Kerr; we were punching lumps out of each other after consuming too much sake at a Japanese restaurant in the hotel. I always loved Paul. On 18 August, we were in Milwaukee, Wisconsin at the Mecca Auditorium for our show. I remember seeing all our trucks lined up inside the venue. I wandered about smoking before the show, in a reflective daze, thinking: *How long will this lifestyle last?*

On the 19th we were at the Civic Hall in St Paul, Minnesota. We were a motley crew, living like pirates as we sailed our good ships-on-wheels through deserts and mountains, forests and plains. We went overnight again to Cincinatti, Ohio. It was now 20 August, and we had another day off. I went out to buy some shoes, and a pair of football boots. We had a game of football arranged with MTV on 24 August in Denver, Colorado, and I had to have real boots for the game. What a downer for me, because the only boots I could find at that time, was a pair of Adidas Celtic, and I, being a red-hot Glasgow Rangers man, was gagging at the thought of having to wear them, but I swallowed the bullet and bought them anyway. Of course, I threw them away right after the game, and asked for forgiveness. I did, however, buy a pair of black and white spats. Malcolm Foster was going to buy them, but I beat him to them.

The next day we played Cincinnati. It was great, really great. After the show I met up with my old American girlfriend, Jeannine Champe, whom I had known from my days in Spain. She came back to the hotel with her friend, who Charlie entertained. We were a good bit tipsy, so I got naked and climbed out of the hotel window. We were about ten storeys up and I held onto the frames and bricks while walking to Charlie's window. Charlie and the girl were totally shocked at my inane stupidity, but I was fearless, having been a painter and decorator in my past life. One slip and I would have been a stain on the sidewalk.

We moved on to Kansas City for another shed gig. It was strange going to these gigs, as they all looked identical, still it's better than stripping wallpaper off a house wall in Priesthill in Glasgow. Next day was the football match between the Treebenders and the Gorbals Diehards. On a pitch in the middle of Denver, Colorado, the city one mile high. The air was thin up there, and running was difficult. We had an old friend from the Average White Band and Paul McCartney's band to referee the game, Mr Hamish Stuart. The game was recorded for MTV. Spoiler alert: it ended in a draw.

The next two days saw us playing at the sensational venue made famous by U2, Red Rocks Amphitheatre, which was about another half a mile further up than the already high Denver, Colorado. If we couldn't catch our breath at the football game the other day, this was very different. What an astounding venue, very spiritual. I think the gods were watching us from up there. The audience were obviously acclimatized by this time, but Mel George Gaynor suffered during one of the shows, almost collapsing during one song, and the paramedics had to be called into action. They administered oxygen, and we all giggled like daft schoolboys. From that moment on, he was named the Oxygen Monster, so cruel were we. After two gigs, we got to breathe easy in Denver (almost; we were still a mile high).

On 27 August we had a day off, so Mick, Charlie, Mel and I hired a car to drive up through the Rockies. We were going to see if we could get a room at The Stanley Hotel in Estes Park. Why there? This is the hotel used for the imaginary Overlook Hotel in *The Shining*. This is where Stephen King wrote the book, and the hotel didn't disappoint. As we walked in, it was quite small, but the walls were covered with early 1930s' black and white photographs of days and events gone by at the Stanley Hotel. By the time we got there it was early evening. There were a lot of old people there, and a band in suits. Mel got up and did a guest spot on drums with these old jazz musicians. We invited some of the old ladies to dance. Sugar grannies, all diamonds and dentures, but not at all like the lady in the bath in Room 237. Although the Overlook Hotel was a fictitious hotel, the Stanley was reported to be haunted, and lots of guests would testify to this. We tried to get rooms, but they were fully booked, so, a few more drinks and a dance, then we board our chariot and hurtle down the mountain pass towards Boulder, Colorado. When we arrived in Boulder, we stopped at a go-kart centre, and raced about like madmen. I pulled the accelerator cable for more speed and was asked to leave by the officials looking after the place, shame on me. When the racing was finished, we headed back to our hotel in Denver.

We next played at Lawlor Events Centre in the heart of Reno and stayed at the MGM Grand Hotel on the Strip. We met up for drinks and a wee flutter in the casino, followed by some wholesome American food before crashing into our rooms for a good sleep.

Then we turned west and headed for one of my favourite cities in America, San Francisco. Two nights at the Greek Theatre in Berkeley, the 31 August and 1 September. Stunning venue; you could swear you were in ancient Greece.

Soon this tour would be over, and we wanted to go out with a bang. We played for two nights at the Pacific Amphitheatre in Costa Mesa on 4–5 September. This was a relatively new venue. The amphitheatre was opened by Barry Manilow in June 1984, so we were playing in the inaugural year, whoop de do dah! You cannot fault the enthusiasm of an American audience; it's a deep joy to perform for them. I remember us all sitting at the hotel having a drink when one of Chrissies' pals was sitting with us, being loud and a bit over the top. I went into a Gene Wilder rant from the film *The Producers* and started joking with her. Unfortunately for me she didn't take it well and she jumped on me, when I started my routine, 'Fat, fat, you fat fatty.' Eventually she sussed that I was re-enacting part of a film, which luckily for me, she had seen.

The tour was over. We made our way to New York for a bit of a rest before flying back to Blighty.

Next on the agenda were gigs in Japan. We travelled there with the Pretenders, we never supported them there. We played two gigs at the Nakano Sun Plaza Hall in Tokyo. I told my guitar tech Andy Battye that I didn't want to drink alcohol at this gig, so if he could put some water out for me, that would be great. Now I don't drink usually when I am gigging, but I will go for one drink if things get hot. So midway through the gig I go and take a big gulp of the water. I nearly choked! By the time I began to swallow, I realised that this was not ordinary water, but sake. Andy fell about laughing, and it wasn't long before it hit me. I flicked up some balloons on stage, and the Japanese audience applauded. Japanese gigs are a holiday for the crew as they are shadowed by a Japanese crew, who then take over every gig while we are playing shows. They take notes of where everything is placed, where plugs are situated, and which leads go where. If you left a half-smoked cigarette on your amp, it would be there every single night, such was their attention to detail. The two gigs were played on 11–12 September, and they were well attended. One thing that was different to Western gigs was the use of a stage curtain. We would go onstage, curtain closed, and you could not hear a pin drop. We questioned ourselves, beginning to think that there was no one there. The curtain rose, and the place was packed: raucous applause and then complete silence, and then we started to play. Very strange, but you get used to it.

We had a day off on 13 September, and Mr Udo, the promoter, invited us all for a meal. The starter was bees in honey. Imagine a dead bee on a windowsill, drenched in honey. I ate one and a half bees, which almost made me chunder. Next up, jellyfish. Oh yummy. Sake and more sake was the biggest order that night. We went from Tokyo to Osaka, to play Mainichi Hall.

We woke up on the 14th to a shuddering room. I thought my girlfriend was jumping on the bed, but she awoke and ran to the door, wedging it open. She knew what to do in an earthquake, as doors can jam shut if the building starts to buckle. Everyone assembled in the reception area. All the bands and crew were there. The earthquake subsided and things got back to normal. Both bands played their gigs, and it was amazing. The next gig was in Nagoya at the Shikokaido Hall.

Japanese fans are so special. They would give us nice presents to take home with us. I studied Japanese from this tour on, and I got quite good. It wasn't till 1995 that my Japanese would improve tenfold. I joined a band called Addict of the Tripp Minds. The band were from Tokyo, and I played at one of the Halls in the Love District. I was the only Gaijin, which means 'foreigner'. There were 5,000 screaming girls, all swooning over Kenichi Okamoto, our singer, who just happened to be a soap star in Japan. I think around five people looked at me at that gig. I appeared gigantic and my white blonde hair was so unusual, I think I frightened the Japanese audiences. I digress.

The Nagoya show, the last show, the finish of this tour went really well. We had about five days off at the end of the tour. I went to Hakone and stayed overnight. The train, the Romancecar, was incredibly fast and luxurious. On my return to Tokyo, I sat with Bruce Findlay and had cinnamon toast. I bought a great wee robot from a shop in Shinjuku. You could programme it to come into your room and wake you up in the morning. I hadn't taught it to build a joint yet, but there was going to be a lot of time for that over the horizon.

We flew back home, first class – just the ticket. Great to be able to stretch your legs and get a proper sleep after our marathon tour. The next event for us was to go to the big John Giblin's studio at Barwell Court, Surrey, to write songs for the new album. It is now October 1984.

Hey, hey, hey and *la, la, la*

In the studio, Mick, Charlie and I listen to the demo from Keith Forsey for 'Don't You Forget About Me'. Jim is reluctant to do the song. We agree that we should be doing our own song, but that is not an option. After discussing all the alternatives, even suggesting that I sing the song, I have a talk with Jim, and I eventually get him to change his mind. He agrees to do it. I must give credit where credit is certainly due, regarding Jim. If it weren't for Jim, we wouldn't have the *hey, hey, hey*s at the start of the song, and also the *la, la, la, la*s at the end. It was a touch of genius, to which can only be attributed to Jim and the cosmos. We recorded it at a studio in Wembley on a dark winter's night. Back to Barwell Court where we worked on 'Oh Jungleland', 'All the Things She Said', which we had written at the Chapel Studios in South Thoresby. 'Ghost Dancing' which we worked out for the upcoming gigs at Barrowland. 'Sanctify Yourself', 'Come a Long Way', 'Once Upon a Time' and possibly 'I Wish You Were Here'. I wrote on all of these tracks, but the track that really boosted this album was 'Alive and Kicking' and I had absolutely nothing to do with it.

Don't You Forget About Me

We had three gigs at Barrowland as we trundled into a new year. It is now 1985. The shows were fantastic. Girls were being pulled out of the audience as they were fainting and being crushed. Bono got up with us one night and sang with the band on 'New Gold Dream'. I really like Bono; he is a gentleman. We stayed at the Beacons Hotel for the three nights, which is now the Holiday Inn. My girlfriend brought her

German shepherd, Kane, to our hotel. We had gathered there to watch the new video we had made for 'Don't You (Forget About Me)'. I complained in front of everybody that the bass player in the video could have been anyone as I wasn't featured as much as the rest of the band. This didn't go down well. The excuse was that I didn't look happy in the video. I thought I was being mysterious, but egos were beginning to be getting the better of some people.

Always On My Mind

We were back in Barwell Court. The songwriting was taking shape. Jim had invited his adopted brother, Joe, down with some family for dinner at the studio. I was going to London for a birthday dinner with my girlfriend and her friends. Again, this didn't go down well with Jim. He had previously said to me in the studio that we were going to try starting the songs with another instrument and not the bass. I knew there was something on his mind.

That night, I shouldn't have driven as I had been drinking. I had an argument with my girlfriend, and then crashed the car into a lamp post. The whole incident ended up in the newspapers, including a photo of my girlfriend topless. She said to me that her agent had made her do the photo.

I drove Jim Kerr back to see Chrissie, as we were finished in the studio for now. He was cheery and quizzing me, asking if I was alright. That was the last time I would see him for at least a year.

I met up with my girlfriend in Glasgow, and all seemed fine with her; in fact, we stayed together on and off for the next couple of years.

Then I got a call from the Simple Minds office, asking me to come in and see them. I was staying with Mick and Hannah at the time, so I left for Edinburgh to go to the office. I walked in, saw Bruce Findlay the manager, and I said, 'What is it, am I sacked?' Bruce looked up and said ,'Yes.'

Charlie, Mick and Paul Kerr, Jim's brother, came into the office. Charlie and Mick were both crying, and Paul was raging about Jim, who was not there. I ended up talking to Jim on the phone. Jim just wouldn't listen or give me a chance to redeem myself.

I had disappeared from the band too often, giving too much attention to my girlfriend, and not nearly enough to the band. But, whatever the reason, I was sacked and that was it.

There was a feeling of screaming silence in my head in the days and weeks that followed. I felt completely alone, and my mates were nowhere to be seen. It was the strangest of feelings to wake up in the morning expecting to see everyone sitting around the table at breakfast … and then reality bites. There's nobody there, no Charlie, no Jim, no Mick and no Mel. Just memories. If it weren't for my dog, Kinski, to care for, I would have been completely lost.

I had recently bought a farmhouse called Craigmarloch in Kilmacolm, with stables, 12 acres of fields, an ornate lawn and gardens, orchard and a large vegetable patch. The house had a huge music room, swimming pool, sauna, sunroom, big kitchen, variety of bedrooms and a garage with two cars, all surrounded by a substantial wood. I would have given that all away in a heartbeat just to be back in the band, I had put my heart and soul into it.

John Giblin, my big pal, came up to see me at the farmhouse and we walked into one of my fields for a heart-to-heart. Jim had offered him my job. John said that if I didn't want him to take the job, then he wouldn't. John was a pal, and a real gentleman. I told him that if anyone was going to take my job, then I would be honoured for it to be him. We parted friends. To the victor, the spoils.

Things were about to take a turn for the better for me. Some heavyweight musicians were coming to my rescue. However, before I tell you about this, let's go back in time.

2. When Harry Met Betty

My father, Harry, played the mouth organ. My mother, Betty, took dance lessons. They met during the Second World War. My mother had all sorts of jobs throughout her life. She worked as a grocery assistant, a chemist assistant, a home help, a nurse at Hampden Park for the Scotland football games; she worked in the wig department at Lewis's – and she even worked at the Odeon Glasgow treating hysterical and fainting teenagers at a Beatles concert in the early 1960s. She was quite a character.

My father worked as a grocery delivery boy. He told me about being knocked down by a tram at Anniesland Cross in Glasgow while on his bike, being caught in the 'coo catcher' at the front of the tram. He would work the canals with his Uncle Bill, pulling barges full of barrels along the canal with huge Clydesdale horses. He played football with his pals in the back courts of Townhead. His grandmother, my great-grandmother, was Annie Edmunds Forbes, a fiery but kind woman. She would make up 'pieces' (sandwiches) for the boys playing football in the back court of the houses. One of the boys became famous in the world of motor cars, a young Arnold Clark.

As a child, my dad had to have six bones removed from each foot. When the war came, he didn't pass the medical, so he joined the Home Guard and became a sergeant. (Dad's Army, yup). His job was to patrol the Gorbals area of Glasgow, just south of the River Clyde. He patrolled the streets with a private who only had a broom handle as a weapon, and my dad, because of his rank, was the only one allowed a rifle – with one round in it. I think keeping order in the Gorbals at that time would have been terrifying – it was a very hard and lawless place – but my dad was a bit of a dark horse, a lovely man, great manners, and hard as nails. You had to be in those days.

One chance he had to do his bit in the war was when he was on anti-aircraft (ack-ack) duty, as German bombers flew over and bombed Clydebank, Glasgow. He received his medal just before his 80th birthday and died before he reached 81.

My mother's father was in the army and as a child she moved around Britain with her sisters, going to different schools. She went as far away as Margate and as close to Glasgow as Ayr, where she was dux of the school. After the war, the family settled in Possilpark, Glasgow. That's where Harry met Betty and their life began together.

Harry and Betty had three children. Elizabeth Ann Forbes, John Henry Forbes and me – I was the youngest, born 3.40 p.m. in the Rottenrow Maternity Hospital on 22 June 1956. I was a breech baby; my mother had to stay in hospital for the last three or four months of her pregnancy and I was eventually delivered by caesarean section. The doctor, at one point, said to my father that there was a chance of losing me or my mother. We both survived.

My earliest memory is sitting up in my pram, crying for my mother outside the Tormusk shops in Castlemilk. She had gone into the grocers, and I couldn't see her. I remember the panic vividly. We were living at 202 Ardencraig Road, Castlemilk, at that time, having moved from 60 Roystonhill, where I spent the first six months of my life, fending off double pneumonia in our 'single end'.

Castlemilk was one of the new projects or overspill areas of Glasgow to accommodate families who had lived in the inner-city slums, which were old, overcrowded tenement buildings with outside toilets and coal bunkers. It's no wonder I contracted double pneumonia. We were now living in a clean, modern, new building with a bathroom, kitchen, garden and three bedrooms. I remember seeing deer in our garden in those early days. At 14 months old I had to go to hospital, as I needed an operation for a double hernia. The old lucky white heather strikes again.

A very young Derek

I had the operation and all that remains of that memory are two scars: white crosses, one on either side above my bollocks.

Our house was right across from Cathkin Braes, which was old farmland with the remains of farm buildings long gone and great sweeping pastures and plains along with old forests and woodland. There were little burns (streams), and if you carried on up and through the woods you would eventually come to two reservoirs – the big resy and the wee resy – and more woods and pastures green.

John, my big brother, as a kid, was always building huts and dens and stuff. He became a joiner when he left school. My father and John built a tree hut. I walked over – I must have been school age – and looked up when a plank he was using slid off the tree and hit me on the head. My dad picked me up and took me back home. I was alright, though.

I was and have always been, from a young age, a devout lady's man. Rosemary Cluney, a girl I fell for near our house, was my first crush. It lasted for about three minutes. My love of the opposite sex caused me a great deal of pain a number of times in my life. One day when I ran

On the veranda on dad's moped

through the woods at the back of my house, chasing a girl that I liked – we were very young – I tripped and fell knee-first onto a broken bottle. The base of the bottle had one big shard of glass pointing upwards, which I managed to fall on with force. It plunged into my leg just below the knee and the blood shot out all over the place. My dad took me to the Victoria Infirmary, and I had three stitches to bring the wound together. I still have the scar to this day, as a reminder not to chase after women.

In Glasgow in the '60s, gang activity was commonplace – and even during this young part of my life it wasn't too far away. I remember gangs of young boys fighting each other in the streets. They came from Ardencraig Quad and were known as the Quaddies. I remember boys filling paper bags with stones and wetting the bag before throwing them. The idea behind it was that the bags would burst open like a two-bob grenade and rain down on the heads of the small combatants.

During these shows of strength, no one was hurt, luckily; it was all a child's game at this stage. One of my school friends who had joined in with the fighting was Andy McCartney, who became a great friend to me later in my musical life.

* * *

Andy went on to work with Cher as her lighting man. He had married one of Bette Midler's backing singers, a lady called Frannie, and they moved from Glasgow to Los Angeles into a beautiful beach house in Malibu. Andy invited me to his house, and Tina Waters of Trinifold Travel was working with Simple Minds as our tour travel agent at this time. It was Tina who helped me pass my driving test. She booked a driving test for me in Hollywood, of all places! She took me to the test centre, where I sat my theory test, which was easy. The practical test was basically to drive up and down, turn a few corners, reverse the car and then park. The examiner asked me if I was Irish, and I replied no, Scottish, and he started speaking in a fake Scottish accent. 'You'll be taking a wee left turn here, laddie'; 'Och that wiz braw, ye ken.' I passed, and it was one of the funniest mornings I'd had in a while.

Andy met up with me again in Melbourne, Australia in the mid '80s when I was on tour with Simple Minds, and he was touring with Cher.

The lovely Tina Waters moved to Glasgow and kept her travel company going. She married an acquaintance of mine, Dougie Souness, manager of the band Wet Wet Wet.

3. Young Derek

Growing up, I always had a real interest in music. My cousin, Lesley Corson, taught me how to play the harmonica and I remember first learning 'The Grand Old Duke of York'. I formed a band with my pals Brian Gray, Alex Gray and Paddy Boyle from school. One of my best mates from school who came along and played the accordion occasionally was Stef McIntyre. We played songs like 'The Lion Sleeps Tonight', 'Wild Thing' and even 'Lili Marlene', which my mother had suggested and which was one of the biggest hits of the Second World War in both the Allied and the Axis camps. We named ourselves the Tiny Troggs. Girls from the houses around us came to watch, listen and 'scream' … it was surreal.

After that, I got more into football. I formed a team called Castlemilk Rangers and we played other kids from the area. A well-known young man from the next close to me was Johnny Lindsay. Johnny had some form of special needs, but that didn't stop him making friends easily. He loved to go to all the games with Rangers, and he took me to the home games and occasionally away games too. He was a friend to anyone who loved the Rangers. We would take the Number 34 bus from the Bundy in Castlemilk Drive to Mosspark Boulevard at Bellahouston Park, then walk down Dumbreck Road till we reached the junction of Dumbreck Road and Paisley Road West, then past the Ibrox House pub on the left and straight on to Ibrox Stadium on Edmiston Drive. We were walking towards the Stadium one day and we were early. I heard someone walking behind me – and it was one of the Rangers players. I was just a young boy, and my hero, Willie Henderson, was walking behind! I turned and said, 'Hello, Willie, can I have your autograph?' He said nothing and walked on. I asked again and still no reaction. I said, 'Mr Henderson, could I have your autograph please?' Still nothing. Then two boys about the same age went up to Willie and said, 'Willie, can we have your autograph?' He stopped and signed for them. I was gutted. I had Willie's book and watched him at Rangers all the time, I never knew why he ignored me. When I left Castlemilk in 1971, Johnny continued to take other pals to the games.

It was 1970 when I went on the school cruise on the ship the SS *Uganda*, built on the River Clyde in 1952, which became a cruise ship between 1968 and 1982. She went on to perform as a hospital ship in the Falklands War. There were a few schools from Glasgow onboard. We were in Stanhope dormitory with the boys from Crookston Castle School in Pollok. Little did I know at that time that my dad would switch from a grocer to a school janitor and that we would move to Crookston Castle School the following year. I liked a girl onboard from Crookston Castle. I still remember her name was Jane Johnston, but I never plucked up the courage to speak to her.

The cruise took us from Greenock to the Azores in the middle of the Atlantic Ocean. We had dolphins following the ship, and after dinner that night I went outside in the dark and watched the water sparkle from the ship's lights. I heard a slapping and looked down nearer the edge of the boat and saw flying fish. They raced alongside the ship. This, to a 14-year-old kid, was quite cool.

One night an older boy from Crookston put some shoe polish in my eye for a laugh. I was upset, so the whole of the Crookston Castle boys grabbed the perpetrator and covered him in polish, including his Albert Halls. They called me the Mad Bull because if anyone's locker wouldn't open, I would charge at it with my head and burst the door open. What an idiot; so much for heading footballs! The song blaring out everywhere at that time was 'All Right Now' by Free.

We left the Azores with a great departing ceremony to the sound of bagpipes. We were heading to the island of Madeira and its capital Funchal. Another coach trip was on the cards, and we ended up on top of the second-highest cliff in Europe. There was an iron fence to stop people falling over, but the safety measure didn't pertain to me. I saw some lizards and I jumped over the fence, holding on while trying to catch one of them. My mates were horrified. I didn't fall – but nor did I catch my prey.

Next stop, the north coast of Africa and Morocco. After a day of cruising, we docked at the port of Ceuta. The order of the day was to haggle with the merchants when buying goods. I wanted a fez for my dad, so I asked the vendor how much. He said ten shillings. I said no, all I will pay is eight. He said no sale, ten or nothing. I agreed to ten shillings but gave him eight. He was none the wiser.

The minibus took us to the edge of the desert, where we met up with the other guys from our school and Crookston and sat on the sand, waiting until we were ushered back to the ship. We declined the camel rides. Fuck me, was it hot. You couldn't walk on the sand with bare feet. Back on the ship we had dinner and dancing, and our next port of call was our last before home: Lisbon. I couldn't wait for that. One of my football heroes played for Benfica: Eusébio da Silva Ferreira, the Black Panther.

I played with a team in the Gorbals area of Glasgow, called Liverpool Boys Club – and Bill Shankly, the Liverpool manager and fellow Scot, supplied us with our football kit. Our coach was Ian McPhee, who had played Inside Left for St Johnstone in the '60s. He would always pick me for the team, but Alby Robertson, our manager and later Kenny Dalglish's father-in-law, would use me as a sub. One game against the league leaders, St Luke's, was most memorable for me. Our home pitch was at Fleshers Haugh in Glasgow Green, where the first-ever Rangers match was held in 1872 against Callander Thistle. Our game against St Luke's started with a goal against us. Just before half-time I scored from the right side about 18 yards out and made it 1–1. Almost straight away St Luke's scored again: 2–1 at half time. We went on for the second half and came off losing 10–1. I went on to become striker coach at Callander Thistle in my fifties!

At the age of 14, I still hadn't picked up a guitar.

After school, I would get driven out to Kirkintilloch by my Uncle Gordon on a Wednesday, to stay overnight with my cousins Ian, Lesley and Shelagh. When I got to my cousins' house we would listen to records, usually the Beatles, and learn songs. I still wasn't playing guitar at this point, but now I had got the bug. Ian was an amazing bass player, and also played guitar. So, at this time I was asked to join his band, which consisted of Billy Costello on lead guitar, Charlie Lumgair on drums, Ian on bass guitar and me as lead vocalist. We rehearsed at a hall in Kirkintilloch in 1970. Some of the songs I sang included 'Good Golly, Miss Molly' and 'All Right Now'. I loved it. Lesley, meanwhile, would teach me more harmonica tunes. The following year we were going to do a show at my school with our wee band named Sgt. Pepper. It never happened. I can't remember why.

I got the chance to buy an acoustic guitar from a friend in Castlemilk called Frannie Shields. It was a Dallas Arbiter acoustic, a subsidiary of Fender, and it was £1, including a case. A pound was a lot of money in

1971, but my mother made the best investment of my life for me. I had the guitar in my hands, and I attempted to play tunes on one string only. I learned 'Love Like a Man' by Ten Years After and 'Badge' by Cream, then it was onto 'The Green Manalishi' by Fleetwood Mac. On Sundays we would go to my grandparents' house in Possilpark, where there was an upright piano in the living room. I would dabble with it, fascinated by the sound – and so clearly enjoying it. My grandfather commented on me being very musical. He was an old soldier, and had been a piper in the Royal Scots Fusiliers. There's some great footage of him in Burma (now Myanmar) at Pinwe, with Mountbatten's Forgotten Army, the Fourteenth, leading the troops along the Burma Railway, built by prisoners of war captured by the Japanese during the Second World War. The Pathé News footage shows the battalion marching behind him while he plays 'The Black Bear' on his bagpipes. He once offered me his bagpipes, but I didn't want him to give them away, so I never accepted them.

Back in Possilpark, my uncle and aunty would always be there! My Uncle John MacLean was a guitar and banjo player, and his wife, my Aunty June, played banjo too. They were very much into the folk scene and had played theatres all over the place. My Aunty June was engaged to a famous Glasgow banjo player, and she was with him when he bought his first banjo. My Uncle John was also a good friend of this famous banjo player. I don't know whose stag night it was – it may have been banjo man's marriage to Iris – but John and the banjo player ended up steaming drunk and sleeping on my grandparents' bed in the house in Possilpark. The banjo player's name was Billy … Billy Connolly!

My Uncle John wrote out 12 simple guitar chords for me – and this was the start; this was what lit the touchpaper for me to have a career in music. I thank him for that with all my heart! I put the guitar down after two weeks with my fingers shredded, and never touched it again for six months. There was a good reason for this and I'll tell you about this later.

In April that year our school had a skiing trip to Austria. My mother found the money and paid for my two-week trip to Söll, a small village in the Austrian Alps. Of course, before going to Austria I had to learn to ski. Two teachers, Mr Jimmy Paul and Mr Aitken, took me and another couple of boys to the Glencoe Ski Resort, where we learned the basics, and after a few visits we were ready for anything.

On the day of the trip, we met at school and were taken to Central Station in Glasgow for the sleeper train to London. We were sleeping on seats in the end, but who could sleep? The excitement was reaching to hysteria! Our flight to Munich was early morning, and this was my first ever flight. After landing, we headed on a coach up into the mountains just over the German border, along roads with beautiful snow-capped pine trees until we arrived in Austria. There were cigarette machines in the streets, and I didn't waste any time getting a packet; not that I smoked at that time, but I was trying to look cool. We were allowed in the pubs and served beer in steins (two-litre mugs). I made a beeline for some English girls who were on a school trip, hooking up with a lovely girl called Julie from Scarborough. Her family owned a pub called the Red Lion. Our teachers, who were slightly pissed, were trying to herd us back to the hotel that evening, it was hilarious.

Next day, we had a full day's skiing. I was skiing downhill and fell over, not for the first time. One of my pals, Boris McGibbon, shouted 'Keep yer heid doon' because he was heading for me at a rate of knots and couldn't stop. I looked up and said, 'Whit?' and he skied over my face, breaking my nose.

When we boarded our coach for the journey home, I went up to one of the teachers who was sitting at the front and said, 'Miss, I think I've broken my nose.' She replied, 'Oh! So, you have.' And that was that.

When I got home, my brother John asked what had happened to my nose. I told him about Boris and asked him to punch it to straighten it. He said, 'No, away ye go, am no' punching it.' I kept on until he gave up and punched me a beauty right in the face. My nose hadn't moved a jot.

Mother and son, 1971

Within a couple of months, we moved house to Pollok, and before we left we had a family holiday to Dennis's caravan site in Scarborough. I was delighted because it meant I could meet up with my girlfriend, Julie, from the skiing holiday. I took a bus out to the Red Lion. It was great to see her, but as with many holiday romances, we soon parted ways.

Dennis's caravan park was also a haunt of the Kerr family. Jim told me that he would have been there with his family round about the same time as us.

My last memory of that holiday was running past a swing park in the dark of night to go to the cliff's edge for a better view of Gristhorpe Bay, and I heard my brother shouting out 'Bean ... get tae fuck!' as he was entertaining a lovely young lady in the long grass.

'Bean' was my brother's nickname for me following a visit to Nat the Barber. We went in, Nat asked who's first, and John pointed to me. I told him I wanted a Bernard's haircut, and he nodded as if he knew what the fuck he was doing. Out came the clippers and he scalped me right into the wood. My ears were sticking out like a taxi with its doors open when he'd finished. Nat turned to John: 'Are you next?' John said: 'No fucking chance,' and left money for my haircut and bolted out the door in hysterics. John said I looked like Plug, a character from *The Beano*, and christened me 'The Beano Kid', shortening it to 'Bean'.

It was my final months at school, and I was approaching my 16th birthday. I had travelled up to Castlemilk from Pollok to see my mates. We went to Rutherglen to the Off Sales to buy some drinks, usually a couple of bottles of cider and a half-bottle of Eldorado, a fortified wine, which tasted shithouse. We got the bus back up to Castlemilk and walked about Ardencraig Road. We drank most of our 'carry-oot' and were standing at the corner of Castlemilk Drive when a gang of youths approached us from further up the drive. They ran at us, shouting: 'Wild Team' and everyone ran – except me. I wasn't a fast runner, so I stood my ground. I knew these guys, so surely they wouldn't mess with John Forbes' little brother. They didn't recognise me until after the skirmish. One of them, 'Snowy', grabbed my hair and tried to boot me in the face, but I blocked his kick, and he broke two fingers in my left hand. I ended up with a plaster cast on my arm and thought my guitar-playing days would be over. That's why I couldn't touch the guitar again for months.

My parents, my sister Elizabeth, brother John and I were taking a break beside the sea in Dunoon for a wee holiday before I started my apprenticeship as a painter and decorator in August. We also took my best pal, Ian Reekie, who was starting his plumbing apprenticeship in August. It was at this time that Eric Clapton's Derek and the Dominos had released 'Layla' and it was never off the radio. I loved it, and I listened to the guitar part intently. I was starting to work out where to put my fingers to play the riff in my mind! I still had the plaster cast on, so all I could do was imagine playing. Like a miracle, though, as soon as the cast was removed, I picked up the guitar and I played the riff, note for note.

In August, I joined up with my painters' squad for my first day as an apprentice painter and decorator. I was given the address to meet up with the tradesmen and the gaffer: Pinmore Street, South Nitshill. The painters' caravan, a big green thing, reeking of turpentine and cigarette ash, was next to Mick MacNeil's house in Craigbank. I asked one of the tradesmen how you get up there to paint the gutters. He looked at me like I was an imbecile and said, 'Stick a feather up your arse and fly up.' It was then I realised that we would be using these huge three splice ladders, doh! During lunch we all congregated in the caravan with our tea cans ready to fill from the urn. I had cheese on my 'pieces'. They asked me where I was from, who got me the job, what my parents did, then that old chestnut: 'What school did you go to?' I said, 'I'm a Protestant,' and the whole van shook with raucous laughter. Typical Glaswegian. You are either a Billy or a Tim. One of the tradesmen was Pat Burns, an ex-football player. He was in the sights of Manchester United and could have signed to them but for breaking his leg at Rosevale Park in a Cup Final, which ended his career. He was the uncle of Tommy Burns, the legendary Glasgow Celtic player, who became the assistant manager of Scotland with Walter Smith and Ally McCoist of Glasgow Rangers, both great friends of mine. Pat Burns would look round at me while painting and he would forget my name. He would go 'hey … eh … mm … eh ARSE FACE!' Which cracked me up every time.

All through my apprenticeship I was learning guitar. I would play every night and all weekend; I was dedicated. I wrote songs and even started a band. We were called Switchback. I started working with a guy called Alistair who lived in Erskine. He was the brother of my best pal Ian Reekie's girlfriend, and that was the connection. He was good, I thought, but our collaboration was short-lived. I got wind of a bass player from Kings Park in Glasgow, called Brian McLintock. Now he was great, a bit whacky; he liked making huge rockets and firing them out of his back garden like a nutty professor. We needed to find another two players for our band. I called my cousin Ian Corson and he agreed to come along as second guitarist, then we found a drummer from Johnstone called Hughie Armstrong, and he had a car! Rehearsals were held in the School Hall at Crookston Castle Secondary, where my father was the janitor. The rehearsals were filmed, but Hughie's wife Isobel threw the film out by mistake (maybe). We borrowed a van from Brian's father's welding shop, and we had our first gig as Switchback in 1973 at the Burns Howff in Glasgow. We stank. We played Led Zeppelin's 'Rock and Roll' in the key of B – and I don't think that Robert Plant could have sang it high either.

4. Better Guitars and Gigs

Practice, practice, practice … my days consisted of working as an apprentice painter, with every spare second devoted to honing my skills as a guitar player. Like a thousand others, I would be listening intently to my favourite vinyl records, attempting to reproduce what I had just heard. A letter arrived on my doorstep, and when I opened it and saw it was a tax rebate, the first thought that came into my head was *I can buy a decent guitar!* I took the bus into Glasgow and headed for McCormack's Music on Bath Street. I found a guitar that was a replica of the Gibson guitar. It was a Grantson SG, and it played well enough for me at the time. This was a good start for me, in the world of better guitars.

> *Note: If you are going to buy a guitar, you must push the boat out for the very best you can afford; it will really speed up the learning. The day you upgrade your guitar, you will be astounded at how much easier playing becomes.*

My sister, Elizabeth, had an Empire Stores catalogue, and in it was a Gibson SG, and I was allowed to pay in instalments. I couldn't help it; I bought that one too. My fingers were burning with the speed I was now playing at. It was early January 1974, and I thought I was a decent player now. It was my second year at Langside College, and I had been asked to play at a concert the College had arranged. I took my new Gibson SG to college with me, as I could practice in my breaks; I was totally obsessed with playing music.

As part of my apprenticeship, I attended college. One very cold wintry day, I took my guitar to college with me, and when I opened the case, the body cracked. I had come out of the freezing cold into the warm hallway of the college – and that was it, the damage was done. I sent the guitar away to be fixed, but never saw it again. It had been stolen. I had a gig to play and had to use my old guitar. It was at this time that I met Jim Kerr; I think this was maybe for the second time. Jim was with his older neighbour, who also loved music, and they would listen to all the cool bands around, like Lou Reed, the Velvet Underground, Genesis with Peter Gabriel, David Bowie, and Cockney Rebel. I remember I was wearing a top hat, white Oxford bags and a red-and-white pinstriped T-shirt with a small leather bomber jacket, and a white silk scarf around my neck, very Mick Ronson! I was in the hallway with my guitar when Jim and Rab McGill appeared with my pal Ian Reekie. I think Jim was well impressed with the way I looked. This, I am sure, planted a seed in the young Kerr's head, and he stalked me until I could be included in his band.

My cousin, Ian Corson, showed me how to play 'Lady Madonna' on his bass guitar. I enjoyed it so much, that I thought bass guitar would be my top second choice. The gig went well, but my nervousness was unbelievable, and I had the worst case of stage fright. It didn't take me long to get used to the gigs and the nerves passed. I was becoming very adept at playing Led Zeppelin songs, both acoustic and electric songs. I was delighted to have mastered 'Over the Hills and Far Away'. Of course, this was just practise for me. I had been writing my own songs for a while, since 1972/73, and I was beginning to feel a need to develop the songwriting side of me.

A wee side note. I bought an Eko 12-string acoustic guitar from the Barras for £40 in the early '70s, and it featured on every Simple Minds

Derek with the Eko 12-string acoustic guitar

album up until *Sparkle in the Rain*, as Charlie didn't have his own acoustic guitar. We went to the Yoker Ferry on the banks of the River Clyde, and filmed us sailing across the water, smiling and laughing away like zoomers. We got enough footage, and when everyone left, we carried on filming the video for 'Speed Your Love to Me', with great helicopter footage of the run down from Ben Lomond and along the length of Loch Lomond. It was stunning. At this stage, 'Waterfront' had only been played on Kid Jensen's radio show which we had recorded a few weeks before at BBC Maida Vale.

Looking back now, I realise that by the time the year 1974 was drawing to a close, I had forged new friendships with like-minded musicians. Kevin Key and Ronnie Costley came into my life, and we formed the band Broad Daylight. We were fans of Free and Bad Company. Broad Daylight never played a gig.

1975 was the year I was in the band Big Dick and the Four Skins. Now, this band played a lot of gigs! You would find us in our band T-shirts in the Doune Castle pub in Shawlands, either playing or drinking. The band included Dicey O'Neil on lead vocals, Duncan Barnwell on second guitar, Brian McLintock on bass guitar, Hughie Armstrong on

Pals from Lloret de Mar

drums and me on lead guitar and vocals. We also had two sets of women backing singers. It was quite a show. I used a violin bow on Zeppelin's 'Dazed and Confused'. We had a ball. I had a new Gibson Les Paul Sunburst Deluxe as my main weapon of music, and there wasn't a song written that I wouldn't attempt.

The band played on into the year 1976. I had seen an advert for a guitarist vocalist in *Melody Maker* – for 10cc. Kevin Godley and Lol Creme had left the band due to artistic differences. I loved the band and could play all the parts easily, so I contacted the band, but never got to audition.

Punk was just around the corner. I was living in a flat with Kevin Key and we were dabbling in a few musical ideas. Kevin loaded my head with all the Frank Zappa that it could hold, and I started to play some of the easier songs from his multitude of albums. My head was full of ideas. 1976 was a good year for me, and better things were to come.

At Doune Castle pub a few friends and I were having a right good swally. I think it was Ian Reekie who told us that a few people he knew were going out to Spain to work the season, and that it would be great if we did it too. Little did Reekie know that he had just lit the fuse: the idea became very attractive and a few months later we were heading there to enjoy the hot sunshine of Lloret de Mar, on the Costa Brava. So, now it was February 1977, and we were in the Doune Castle pub getting ready for our send-off, which consisted of three or four cars driving to Buchanan Street bus station, with lots of our friends, including Cathy Dolan, Maureen Kane, Rita Brown and Marjorie Richardson (the aforementioned backing singers of our band). It was great to be going to Spain, but we knew we would miss our mates.

I spent the next five months in Lloret de Mar, playing in bars, mostly playing guitar but also playing bass guitar for several hours a night, as the bass player in the band couldn't sing and play bass at the same time. This is where my journey into developing my bass playing expanded. Being in Spain was fun, but I became tempted to return home to Glasgow, hearing about a new wave of bands and punk becoming more mainstream.

I arrived back in Glasgow from Spain on 22 June 1977, my 21st birthday. Home was where my parents lived – 76 Dougie Road – and the house was empty because they were on holiday. I didn't even have the price of a pint of lager to celebrate. Not much of a welcome home!

As the months passed, Kevin Key asked if I would play bass with a punk band called Subs. At the time, I was playing lead guitar and I really wanted to continue as a lead guitar player, but I did like playing bass too. Kevin Key and Steve Cheyne were playing guitar in the band and as there was no room for a third guitar player I agreed to join up, getting back behind the four strings and playing bass. Steve became our manager because his guitar playing was the 'talk of the Steamie', sounding like a tractor revving up in the background. The band were great though. The singer, Callum Cuthbertson, now an actor, was an energetic frontman, a force of nature and a thoroughly good chap. Callum resembled Art Garfunkel after a night on the Angel Dust. Our drummer, Ali MacKenzie, was outstanding, and one of the best I had worked with so far. Ali had the timing of a Swiss clock.

Kevin and I, having received some positive responses, went down to London with demos we had recorded at Glasgow's Cava Studios. Brian Young, owner and engineer at Cava, did a great job of recording the tracks and we had the attention of the first punk label, Stiff Records. Dave Robinson, Managing Director at Stiff, put together a tour of London for us. Our first gig was a Stiff/Chiswick challenge at the Royal Albert Hall annex. We played with the band The Members, and we all became good friends.

Our tour of London had some great moments. We played The Red Cow in Hammersmith, where I became pals with John 'Rhino' Edwards, the second bass player of Status Quo. The next gig we played was the Vortex, one of the most famous venues of the punk era. The Hope and Anchor was also special, as our label mates Devo came to the show that night. I saw Mark Mothersbaugh standing watching us. He was smiling away. I turned round to tell Ali, our drummer, that they were at the gig but when I looked back, they had all vanished. We played Stoke Newington next – and guess who was supporting us? Gary Numan with Tubeway Army! We played Rochester Castle too, then played The Nashville, which has been renamed the Three Kings for a good number of years now. We supported Wreckless Eric, who had also been signed by Stiff. It was great playing with the guys from the Blockheads. I got to know Norman Watt-Roy at many a Festival with XSM (Ex-Simple Minds), the band that I started with Brian McGee. A stand-out moment from those XSM days was bringing Tony Donald onstage with us to play bass alongside myself. Tony was the original Simple Minds bass player and a thoroughly nice guy. Unfortunately, Tony (Larry the Lift Man), has joined other legends to play at the great gig in the sky.

The Subs had a studio date with Larry Wallis of Motörhead and the Pink Fairies, among others. We were to record our first single for Stiff Records, and Larry was to produce it. We recorded 'Gimme Your Heart' and 'Party Clothes', a double A-side. It was recorded at Pathway Studios in the Angel, Islington. The studio belonged to the legend John Foxx of Ultravox. The single was a hit, especially in Belgium – my first chart success!

One of our shows was at Clouds in Edinburgh, where we were the headliners. We had the Skids on with us as one of the supports. They brought busloads of people from Dunfermline. Not long after, they were signed to Virgin Records, and they had a lot of success – on the singles front especially. They were a great band, although I couldn't make out a fucking word of what my old pal Richard Jobson was singing!

There were a number of gigs booked for the Subs in January 1978. We made a special trip up to Stornaway, near Ali MacKenzie's ancestral home. We drove from Glasgow and made our way up to Ullapool, the Las Vegas of the North. We boarded the ferry and braved the Minch, the stretch of water between the mainland and the Hebrides. We had the entire band and equipment with us as well as a few friends and roadies who hid in the back of the van to dodge the fare. We played the Town Hall in Stornaway, and everyone loved the show. It was a great turnout that night. As it was only a one-show gig, we got ourselves prepped to leave in the morning. It was a lovely crisp day, peppered with glinting sunshine, and we were heading to a wedding reception as guests, at a hotel at the Port of Ness on the northernmost edge of the Island. The people who invited us had been at the Town Hall the other night and wanted to give us a warm Highland welcome. We were all merry on the whisky and danced for hours with the other guests. It was one of the finest weddings since the Vikings had left the island. Our ferry in the morning was leaving at 6 a.m., so we had to get down to the harbour at Stornaway and managed to grab some shut-eye in the waiting room and van, wherever you could find a space to stretch out.

Overnight, the weather had taken a turn and snow had begun to fall in earnest. The ferry was being tossed all over the place while the brave captain sallied forth. It was one of the most terrifying journeys I have ever made. Or, it would have been if I hadn't still been pissed from the night before. In fact, I managed to sleep most of the way. We arrived in Ullapool to a total whiteout after a night of blizzards. We drove off the ferry with our stowaways intact up into the mountainous terrain ahead. The roads were treacherous, and to make things worse the blizzard started again. We were really struggling to see through the windscreen, until eventually we could go no further. The engine was turned off, and it quickly got cold. Ali remembered there was a cottage that he was quite certain was nearby. He and I elected to go outside in the snow and try to find it. We were up to our waists in snow, making it difficult to walk, to say the least. We reached a fence almost completely buried, so we crawled over the last wire at the top. Through the snowfall we thought we saw smoke, we could smell smoke, that undeniable reek of burning peat. We headed for the cottage. An old lady opened the door and invited us in.

We collected the rest of the band and crew and went up to the cottage. The cottage was owned by an old Air Commodore and his wife, Mr and Mrs Campbell. We were there for several days, and all had to pitch in with chores every day, military style. One of our guys stood to attention, saluting the Commodore every time he was spoken to. The Commodore was impressed. It was Billy Thompson from Castlemilk, the 'acid man' supplier of all things hallucinogenic. The cottage was incredibly well stocked with food – bread, eggs, steak, sausages, venison, as well as alcohol and cigarettes. Cooking duties were shared. We were warm, fed and safe, while outside the snow was still falling heavily. That night, Billy and I went out with shovels and torches to see if anyone else was trapped in the snow. We heard on the radio that a truck was missing near us. We walked towards the main road, shovels up at our faces to fend off the savage blizzard, and got a glimpse of a truck and made for it. Inside the truck was the driver and Roger, the cabin boy from the ferry. They were OK and pleased to see us and we took them back to the cottage. 'Another two for dinner,' said Bilbo. I think we had saved their lives.

The next day the snow stopped, and we went out on patrol again. I think it was Ali who spotted a little dark patch the size of a packet of cigarettes in the snow. He went to check, and it was a lot bigger than he first thought: a Volkswagen Beetle, almost completely buried. We dug the car out to the window level, and inside was an old couple. They had written their will for their children, as they had thought this was the end. Not while the Subs were in town! We got them out, called the emergency services and they were taken to hospital. Another two lives saved! Our exploits were reported in newspapers across the UK. We also received lots of radio and television attention.

At the end of those January days the band had lots of radio and media coverage, but it didn't give our new single the impact we had hoped for. I think it must have been towards the end of February that Ali MacKenzie, our drummer (and lifesaver), decided to move on to pastures new. We had a gig at Strathclyde University, and we needed a drummer. I asked Brian McGee if he would sit in for the gig. He did, and it was a great show. During this time, I had heard that Jim Kerr was often in the audience of a Subs gig. I wonder if, even then, he was lining me up to join his new venture.

5. Simple Minds

In March, I was asked if I would stand in for the original bass player of Simple Minds, Tony Donald. I was all for it, but I did say that I wanted to get back to playing lead guitar. I had been asked to audition for the Rezillos, but although wee Jo Callis wanted me to join after my audition, Fay and Eugene decided against it. They gave the job to a good-looking bastard called Simon Templar. I think I dodged a bullet back then.

Simple Minds wanted me, but I still wanted to get back to playing lead guitar and I thought my days on the bass would be over, but something happened to mess that up one for me. My 1972 Gibson Les Paul (Sunburst Deluxe) got nicked from the office where the Subs rehearsed. I did my best to get it back, but it wasn't until years later that I found out who might have taken it. I would just like to thank the thieving bastard for, were it not for him, I would not have had my contribution to the unmistakeable sound of Scotland's most successful band.

In March 1978 I told the newly formed band Simple Minds that I was all theirs, and I was delighted to join them as their bass player. The line-up at that time was Jim Kerr, Brian McGee, Charlie Burchill, Mick MacNeil, Duncan Barnwell (though Duncan wasn't to last much longer) and me.

First Rehearsal

I was living in an attic flat at 30 Cathkin Road, Battlefield, Glasgow. The flat was a midge's dickie from my old school, Grange Secondary. I left my girlfriend at the flat and made my way to Pollok, Glasgow, where Duncan Barnwell was living with his parents. Duncan's dad was a school janitor and Simple Minds had been using the school for rehearsals. I knew Pollock well because my father was a school janitor too at Crookston Castle Secondary.

At the rehearsal we had the set ready quickly; I'd already learned the parts, having seen the band a number of times. My brain at that time was like a sponge; I was ready for learning new things. The rehearsal seemed to go quite well. Afterwards, I started heading home, taking a shortcut through the backstreets. As I left the streets to take a path, which had a steep embankment of grass and trees, a man about 30 years old approached me holding a bag of chips, and in true Glaswegian style insisted that I take a chip! He was totally pissed. I politely declined and changed the subject by asking what the score was at the football. He mumbled that Rangers had won, got a bit angry and started to advance with his chips, pushing them towards my face. I declined a second time and told him I had to go because my girlfriend was making dinner, which she was, and I was late. I started to climb the embankment and he followed, slipping back down the wet grass. I could hear him shouting after me and I just carried on walking down the lane. Then I heard running and shouting coming from behind me, and he came at me. He went on about the chips, grabbed my T-shirt at the neck and ripped it. I did nothing. He grabbed me again and stuck the head on me, and in doing so hit me right on my front teeth, cutting his forehead. This was the last straw, and he foolishly kicked my guitar case in my hand so that I would drop it, which I did. Nobody kicks my guitar! I turned from calm to bam and said: 'Come here, ya cunt,' and punched him right in the face. I chased him as he ran, and I gave him a right doing. I then tied him to the fence with his scarf and went home. At home I realised he had ripped off my silver chain with a silver guitar on it, so I went back to the lane to try and find it. Luckily, I did. The man was nowhere to be seen. I tried to cool down, but although I have a lot of patience, I'm the first to admit that when the dam bursts I am consumed by a terrible temper.

First Gig The Mars Bar

I think it was a Sunday night and a lot of people had turned up for the show. The band decided to wear make-up, and I joined in with some badly applied eye make-up. I looked like a panda. My girlfriend had bought me some girls' sandals and a couple of satin suits, one pink and one white – I was infatuated with the New York Dolls. On that night I wore a black jacket, the collar up, black trousers and white wedge sandals. I gave my white suit jacket to Jim Kerr. Brian McGee was as flamboyant as the rest of us. I had seen him playing drums in a fur coat before. Charlie looked great, as did Mick. Duncan was cool too with his Gold Top Les Paul. Simple Minds at that time had a brother-and-sister sound and lighting team, David and Jaine Henderson from East

Kilbride. They provided a Perspex head with a spinning blue police light in it! Their father had been a policeman. Without their input, we would have just been another band, albeit great, but the theatrics they provided made the whole show magical. Simple Minds were now becoming more polished and a force to be reckoned with. David had recorded an intro tape for when we came onstage. It was a warped-sounding musical box – incredibly eerie. At the last dying note the band would kick in with 'Act of Love'. What a start!

Every second Sunday, we played at the Mars Bar; Simple Minds had a residency there. We would use our big green bus as the dressing room. It was also perfect for carrying equipment, band and crew. We had many an adventure on the old green girl. We travelled to Perth for a gig at the Isle of Skye Hotel, where lots of bands played in the late '70s. This gig was memorable for an altercation with an older guy in a red and black lumberjack shirt. Brian McGee cheekily spouted his mouth off in a way that didn't go down well, and he was challenged to a fight. The guy charged at Brian, the band jumped in and all hell broke loose. Our manager, Bruce Findlay, calmed everyone down and the gig was good in the end.

We had quite a lot of gigs booked at that time as an unsigned band. I remember a gig at the Stagecoach in Dumfries, where only a handful of people turned up. The whole thing was a disaster and, to top it all, Jim left his jacket in the dressing room where there was an infestation of fleas. He learnt new dance moves that night with his itchy toast rack!

There was always a reliable crowd at the Mars Bar and the gigs were always rammed. Luckily, we could park the Green Goddess in the lane beside the fire exit doors and we would enter this way for the show. On one of these chaotic nights Bruce Findlay and his wife Jane came to see us. Bruce spoke to us after the gig almost in tears; he was blown away. He likened this encounter to the discovery of the Beatles by Brian Epstein at the Cavern Club in Liverpool. Not one for exaggeration, he promised us the world.

One day we met at Mick MacNeil's house in Craigbank, Glasgow. I had to pick up a hired van that Russell Barry had arranged for us for a gig. It wasn't ready in time, so we were late in arriving. Brian McGee came up to the door, complaining. He said: 'That's the last time you will get the van,' and threw his gloves into the van, which hit me in the face. I jumped out and knocked him to the floor. I broke his nose and my finger. *Fuck*, I thought (again), *that's the end of my career*; we had signed

Brian McGee in action

our record deal the week before. Brian and I made up; Mick's mum wondered if he should be mixing with such rough types.

We played Grangemouth a week later, with its New York skyline courtesy of the refinery, which lit up like Manhattan on a winter night. I had ended up with a plaster cast on my right arm and Brian with a big blooter nose. Our faithful roadie, Matt Dunn, got a pair of pliers and bit away the plaster cast to free my fingers for the gig. We played a blinder that night. My white Guild bass guitar was taking a beating from my plaster cast, and I managed to rip the paint off through to the wood. I used my thumb for most of the gig, as that was really the only digit free enough to play the strings. After we were all packed up and our crew were loading the van, we were feeling just a tad hungry. I never ate anything before gigs unless it was at least three hours prior to stage time. We went to the local fish and chip shop, and I bought my first 'white pudding' – who knows what was in it, but with chips and a pickled onion we were sorted.

The gigs in Grangemouth Town Hall were always fantastic. We felt we were knocking on the door and that everything was looking up for

Bruce Findlay, Simple Minds manager

Simple Minds. We were supporting some great bands, including Squeeze (with Jools Holland), and Ultravox at their best, with John Foxx and my great pal Billy Currie. One song I remember playing which went down well at Grangemouth was 'No Cure'.

We were getting to know Bruce Findlay; he was a good manager and became a good friend. We were soon travelling to Edinburgh on a weekly basis to see him at his offices. Simple Minds by this time were now a band of six, but it would not be long before it was honed down to five!

Zoom Records

Bruce Findlay signed us to his Zoom Records label and began to tout our demos to the major labels in London. His hard work paid off: because the American Ben Edmonds, head of A&R at Arista Records, was coming to our show at the Carnegie Hall Annexe in Dunfermline. He'd heard positive things about the band, and was coming with a view to possibly signing us. It was after this show that Duncan's fate was sealed, and it had nothing to do with his musical ability. Ben Edmonds words were: 'OK, guys, I will sign you to Arista Records, on one condition. You need to get rid of the guitar player stage left, he doesn't look the part.' His reasoning was that Duncan looked out of place and he felt that Duncan had not made the effort with his stage appearance and didn't fit in with the rest of the band. Other versions are available. We could have had a word with Duncan, but as this was mostly the Jim and Charlie show, it would be their decision to lose Duncan. The deal offered to the band was more important than keeping Duncan.

Following the visit from Ben Edmonds, I got a call from Jim and Charlie to meet up. They told me that they had gone ahead and sacked Duncan. The first thing I thought was, *if Duncan is going, then I'll go too*. Jim and Charlie told me that Duncan had assumed it was me who was being sacked, because I was going to Blackpool every weekend to see my girlfriend, who was working the summer there. I would get the train back only just in time for the Mars Bar gigs – and the band would be in a state of panic, thinking that I would be late! I never was, luckily! Duncan was prepared to let me go, according to Jim and Charlie. I thought about that and said if Duncan was prepared to go along with me being sacked, then I would do the same for him. Later, when I spoke to Duncan, he told me that Jim and Charlie had said that they would use me until they made it – and then get rid of me too. Anyway, at this point, with Duncan gone, the band was now five.

Now that we had informally agreed with Ben, it was time to speak to the big cheese of the record company. We travelled to London with Bruce for a meet and greet with the staff and bosses of Arista Records. We met everyone working in the offices on Upper Brook Street. We loved the staff – well, most of them. The managing director, Charles Levison, put pen to paper with an offer via Robert White, who was very soon to become our lawyer and assistant manager to Bruce at the world-famous Schoolhouse Management Company. The band drove through to Edinburgh to sign the recording contract at the Caledonian Hotel on Lothian Road, not far from our offices at Shandwick Place in the top floor of Bruce's Records, one of a chain of shops that Bruce and brother Brian owned throughout Scotland.

Under Bruce's wing our live shows began to expand. We played all over Scotland every week, and we played Edinburgh University as well as at established venues like Tiffany's. We had supported Squeeze, Ultravox, Generation X, Siouxsie and the Banshees, and 999, amongst others, while, of course, also playing our own Simple Minds shows.

We rehearsed at a place called Lenny Mains just to the west of Edinburgh. There, we honed the songs from the set list, which at this

Simple Minds

Liza and Robert White, management

time were mainly written by Jim and Charlie. With the introduction of Mick MacNeil and myself into the fold, that was all about to change. Both Mick and I had played with various bands, and both of us had learned through playing lots of different types of venues including working men's clubs. We had tunes coming out of our arse. We both felt that we could add something to the mix.

First Album Flight *Life in a Day*

In January 1979, we flew from Scotland to London to record our first album.

Our equipment had gone on ahead by road to the studio, accompanied by our road crew. We were lucky enough to be going by plane. I was the only one *not* travelling with a belly load of hash, though this would change by the time the album was finished. We were picked up at the airport, by a chauffeur. A huge gold Bentley was purring at the curb, courtesy of Arista. Charles Levison had kindly let us use his car for the duration of the album. It was quite comical the way we would ask the chauffeur to stop so that we might go into an off-licence to load up with a cargo of sweets and alcohol. We passed men working on the road, and one of us cheeky young bastards shouted out, 'Get tae yer work!' Outrageous, but we were just five hairy-arsed boys!

We were taken to the Farmyard, a recording studio in Little Chalfont, near Amersham, England. The studio was recommended to us by Mick McKenna, who engineered the Rolling Stones mobile recording truck, with a sixteen-year-old Mariella Frostrup as tape operator. The driver of the Rolling Stones mobile was a guy called Pete the Fish, so-called because he was one of the diving team with Jacques Cousteau. He was a bit of a character. One day at the Old Mill in Rockfield in the Stones mobile, Charlie Burchill told a really funny joke to Pete the Fish. At the punchline Pete looked away without reacting. Charlie was raging, but it was hilarious to us. From that day on, if anyone was ignored or talked over, that was known as Pete the Fish!

The farmhouse used to be the property of the actor Dirk Bogarde, and later it was bought up by some notable people who were collaborating to convert the farmhouse and outbuildings into a recording studio. At the time of our first album, *Life in a Day*, the studio belonged to Trevor Morais (the drummer who took over from Ringo Starr in Rory Storm and the Hurricanes, when Ringo joined the Beatles) and Trevor's Swedish wife Eve. The studio was made into a proper going concern when Rupert Hine joined the fold, and proceeded to record Howard Jones and Tina Turner (not together, though).

With the studio up and running, they expanded by utilising the many outbuildings. One building was a rehearsal space for the band Brand X. Phil Collins was the drummer, and my longtime friend John Giblin was the bass player. The Rolling Stones mobile now lived at the Studio, so Pete the Fish started making high-quality bass guitars via his Wal Basses, and John 'The Ox' Entwistle, the Who legend and bass god, put his money into this worthy venture. I can tell you that Wal Basses are worth it: I had both a fretted and fretless one with Simple Minds and Propaganda. Later on, I would sell them to a man from Moscow when we met at Checkpoint Charlie in Berlin. From Russia with Love, or with money for two Wal bass guitars!

The encouragement from John Leckie was inspiring. I was happy with my input into the end section of 'Pleasantly Disturbed' and 'Murder Story', which were really shaping up to be standout tracks, especially with the frenzied ending that went down so well for when we performed live. The song 'Life in a Day' was lifted by a guy that I was scheduled to play a few shows with a few years back, but once he knew who I was he disappeared sharpish! The guy had used it for the *Brookside* theme, and we should have stopped him there and then, but we were too inexperienced at that time. 'Chelsea Girl' and 'Life in a Day' had turned out to be the best tracks for singles – well, as voted by the staff at Arista Records anyway.

'Life In a Day', the single, had made it into the Top 75 of the charts – our first hit. 'Chelsea Girl' was next, and it didn't do as well. If I were a gambling man, I'd have put money on 'Chelsea Girl' to have been a huge hit.

We did the video for 'Chelsea Girl' at a studio just off Carnaby Street in London. The son of the actor Stanley Baker was the director. It was quite a quick affair. The great thing about doing the videos was having a load of clothes and shoes bought for you. I had a dark blue suit with lots of multicoloured stitches throughout, bought for me from Johnson's on the Kings Road, Chelsea. One shop that stood out was Sex, a favourite haunt of aficionados of the punk scene, run by Vivienne Westwood and Malcolm McLaren.

Every time we went to London, we would head to Arista. Bruce Findlay, our manager, would accompany us, like a diminutive Gandalf, leading the way and leaving a mixture of mirth and chaos as he swept through the building like a Scottish tsunami. That was one of the great attributes of our Bruce: he could talk the legs off of a centipede. Everybody loved him, including us. There would be moments of genius which exploded from his enormous head. I had to move my own head from side to side like an owl to keep his head in my sight.

The day he was let loose on the office intercom was priceless. It went something like this: button down, microphone on, all offices connected and Bruce in a posh English accent demanding, 'Nicola … Nicola … could you come to my office and tuck my socks … Nicola …' I may be wrong, but it sounded like that at the time!

Any time we had a bad gig, or were feeling down about a show, Bruce would come in and within 30 seconds we were all in stitches laughing at his antics. He was indeed the fifth Beatle – or, rather, given that we were five, the sixth! If someone was being aggressive or annoying any one of us, all we needed to do was to have Bruce open a beer bottle for us with his teeth and watch the aggressor slink away.

Derek Forbes

Charlie Burchill, Arista Records, 1979

The staff at Arista were amazing. Charles Levison was a lovely man, not unlike Alastair Sim. Julie Hooker and Saadia Duckworth were like our big sisters and looked after us. They had experience, having lived through the Bay City Rollers years. Other artists on the books with the company when we were there were Barry Manilow, Patti Smith, Iggy Pop and Lou Reed – not bad for starters! Every time we visited the offices, we were given loads of albums. In later years Julie would come to our shows in New York, where she worked with Paul Simon and looked after his son. She would bring him to our shows too.

On Tour

On 27 March 1979, we drove to the BBC TV Studios on Oxford Road, Manchester. We stayed in an upmarket, no riff-raff hotel in the city centre.

We were to appear for the first time playing live in good old England. We were now feeling that all our hard work in the wilds of Scotland was beginning to pay off. National television, wow! *The Old Grey Whistle Test* – fuck me, this was Big Time. This iconic show had been watched by hordes of young, cool British music fans for years, and it was the Number One music show on TV. I remember sitting watching the show at my house in Pollok, Glasgow, and my dad sticking his head round the door saying, 'Derek, what's that you're watching?' I replied, 'The Whistle Test.' He retorted, 'I could fart a better tune!'

Today, we have Jools Holland and his eclectic electric choice of up-and-coming bands and old legends to keep the flag flying. Oh, how sorely missed is the *Whistle Test*! The alternative then was *Top of the Pops*, where occasionally you would see the Who, Free, Slade, Bolan and Bowie, Roxy Music, Be-Bop Deluxe ... along with a whole load of absolute tripe. There were good DJ presenters like Kid Jensen, Peter Powell, Janice Long, all great pioneers of good music. Do we mention the odd man out, that evil piece of shit Jimmy Savile? I remember the first time we appeared on *Top of the Pops*; Savile was hosting the show. He never came to introduce himself to us, which I thought was bad form.

At the *Whistle Test* we met up with the lovely Annie Nightingale, who was hosting the show that night. Our crew set up the gear and we had a few line and TV checks and a few run-throughs before doing the 'almost live' short set. In those days we swapped clothes quite a lot, and I remember Mick MacNeil was wearing a Bowie-style blue velvet jacket which belonged to Jim Kerr. When Mick played the end part of 'Life in a Day' on the *Old Grey Whistle Test*, the borrowed blue velvet jacket rode up his back as he made a right mess of the ending ... it's there for all to see! Great times. When I saw the profile shot of my broken nose, I thought my career was over there and then. It looked like Donald Fagen of Steely Dan had joined us on bass!

After we finished at the BBC, we went back to the hotel with Annie Nightingale and had a few drinks. She was incredibly funny, and really looked after us. Matt Dunn, our faithful roadie, was charming the pants off her.

One gig we had was at the Astoria, Abbeymount in Edinburgh. By all accounts it wasn't our best show. There was a power cut – a bit of a recurring theme in our travels around the globe. Then, on 30 March, were drove to York for a gig at the Pop Club. This would be our second performance in England, and really our first gig of a full set. I have no recollection of this one; we were just cutting our teeth at this time. We had a small run of gigs to follow starting in the Technical College in Dumfries on 5 April, followed by the Fforde Grene Hotel in Leeds on 6 April. On 8 April we ended up at the Memorial Hall in Newbridge, Wales. This was our first gig in Wales, and it was a great one with a great crowd of people.

We then headed for the first time to Devon to the Grand Hotel, Dawlish, on 11 April. On our way there we had stopped off at Stonehenge. The last gig on 13 April was the 78 Club in Burton on Trent. It was to be the last show before we started the tour with Magazine, and all we could think about then was our first support tour, the tour of our lives, with one of the best bands to come out of the punk era. A band who were streets ahead of most of their contemporaries – but hey, they hadn't met us yet!

Before the tour, our managers, Bruce Findlay and Robert White, and the rest of the backroom staff, arranged a meal for our parents at the Ubiquitous Chip in Glasgow's Ashton Lane. It was the first time that they all had met. It was a great evening and we talked about looking forward to seeing our live performance on the *Whistle Test*, which would be broadcast in the coming weeks.

Magazine, the *Secondhand Daylight* Tour

After our album *Life in a Day* was released, we were heading out on tour with Magazine. We bought an old Volkswagen Camper to be our tour bus; it was tiny, but it had all the horseshit you needed for boiling a kettle and sleeping, albeit awkwardly. We bought the bus from the mother of our lighting team, David and Jaine Henderson. It turned out to be a piece of shit, breaking down just as we arrived at our first support gig with Magazine. So much for nepotism.

The venue was fantastic, the Winter Gardens in Great Malvern. It was 16 April 1979. Magazine were touring with their second album, *Secondhand Daylight*, produced by the one and only John Leckie. We met up with the band and the incredible, theatrical, ex-member and vocalist of the Buzzcocks Howard Devoto. On bass was a man who became an early influence on me, Barry Adamson. The keyboard player, Dave Formula, reminded me of Biffo the Bear from *The Beano*. On drums was a very nice guy John Doyle, who played and sounded like a drum machine. And last, but certainly not least, a diminutive guitar legend from sunny Greenock in Scotland, the one and only John McGeoch, ex-member of the Armoury Show and the brilliant Siouxsie and the Banshees. We went on stage first and went down well, as we had hoped. Our live performances were developing and the reviews appeared mostly favorable.

In these embryonic times of Simple Minds, we were like magpies, collecting ideas from all around us. Jim was really impressed by Howard's mike stand, which had a step on it akin to a ladder. To the audience he must have appeared like a ghost floating up above them. Jim made a call and had a stand like this made for our next tour. The difference was that Jim looked like a Scottish fucker from Glasgow with a bowl haircut.

The following day we managed to get ourselves to King George's Hall in Blackburn. A young and fresh, though rather rubber-faced, young man appeared at the soundcheck. It was none other than Jim's younger brother, Paul. A football player, he had been sent out on loan from Celtic to Blackburn Football Club. I think this was where Paul decided he liked the idea of working in music instead. The next day we played Sheffield Top Rank, soon to be one of our strongest locations, with staunch support from the youth of this steel city.

We had some incredible gigs on that tour. De Montford Hall in Leicester was one that inspired me greatly.

On 23 April we are playing the Apollo Manchester. Magazine was at their best in their hometown, and watching them perform 'The Light Pours Out of Me' that night was incredible, a complete mastery of form, musical awareness and lyrical content. They brought the house down. The Apollo had a great dressing room – probably the best I have ever seen in my musical career. Another contender would be Zeche Bochum, Germany. But back to good old Manchester and Shirley Bassey: she had played there, and anywhere she played she would have the room decorated to her taste. In this case the dressing room was beautifully decked out with a marble fireplace and plush comfortable sofas accompanied by a scattering of ornate tables. The carpet was so thick Charlie nearly got lost in it and we had to throw a rope down to get him out. Charlie had his Carlsbro Stingray amp stolen at that gig after the show. It turned up years later in a pawn shop in Glasgow. I saw it first, but didn't buy it. Mick MacNeil did, and it could be seen at his studio in pride of place.

Our hotel, The Polak, however, wasn't a patch on Ms Bassey's dressing room. The rooms were not the cleanest and, to cap it all, there was a very strange, tall cabinet lurking like an unwanted guest in the TV room. We had been sitting there for a while when, out of nowhere, a man appeared. Wrapped in a towel and carrying a small washing bag, he opened the door of the strange cabinet and stepped in. We heard running water: a fucking shower in the TV room! Before leaving I went into Brian McGee's suite (aye right) and lobbed a pair of smelly socks on top of his wardrobe. This started a global tour ritual of mine that involved leaving abandoned smelly socks in all the hotels we stayed in. You can probably see them from space.

Our first album, *Life in a Day,* had now been released. The tour had been ticking along splendidly until we found out the chart positions for that week. Our album *Life in a Day* was further up the charts than Magazine's *Secondhand Daylight*. Did jealousy, the green-eyed monster, raise its head? We were playing our set onstage at the Theatre Royal, Drury Lane in London and suddenly the power went down. We were still quite inexperienced and didn't know what to do, so we walked off the stage. As the story goes, it was one of the band and/or a crew member from Magazine who pulled the plug. A crew member told us it was 'Raf' and 'Biffo', though it still remains a mystery. If true, though, it was a huge backhanded compliment, and it made us all the more determined to do well. The tour had been sensational, and it sowed the seeds for us to break away from the fragmented sound of the first album and become the Simple Minds band we wanted to be, united in our ideas for the new exciting musical journey.

The tour cantered on into Canterbury and 'May the 4th be with you' – one of the best gigs on the tour at Cambridge Corn Exchange. It was a huge hall, and the stage was not that high, so our interaction with the audience was great, plus we got free popcorn. After all, it was a Corn Exchange. The next show, on 5 May, was Leeds University – back again! I was the proud owner of the inspirational Who album *Live at Leeds,* which was recorded there.

The tour with Magazine was now nearly at the end. We trundled into Liverpool and set up our gear onstage for the last time, at the Liverpool Empire. I was delighted to be playing on proper Beatles ground. I was, and I still am, a huge Beatles fan and stepping onto the stage of the Liverpool Empire for me was very special indeed. As a teenager in the '60s, my dearly departed sister Elizabeth was in her room with her friends playing Beatles records all day long. I can still picture it now; so many memories.

In Liverpool, we stayed at the Adelphi Hotel and I shared a room with Mick. We opened our window which faced towards the back of the restaurant kitchen. There were some pots lying around the back door with peeled potatoes in them. We had a competition to see who could throw one of our socks into the pot. Of course, we got one in, and closed the window in panic lest we be caught. It was a great show, great to tour with Magazine and a real true taste of what else was coming our way as a band.

Back on Tour Again – and it's still 1979

Two days later, on 8 May, we were back onstage in our hometown Glasgow, at the Art School. We then had a short time to write new material and rehearse for a gig at Tiffany's Edinburgh on 21 May. We played there a couple of times. Once we supported Johnny Kidd & the Pirates and once a rockabilly band, probably Matchbox. This was our time to shine. A great performance, according to fans. It was now time to go to an old holiday haunt of mine, Ayr, to play our first ever gig there at the Pavilion, on 23 May. That was a memorable night. The show itself was as good as it gets, and afterwards we signed autographs for about two hours to what seemed an endless stream of people. Next stop, 26 May, was in Aberdeen at the Music Hall – and this time as the headline act.

We had played Aberdeen a lot in the past, once as support to the Stranglers. What a day and night that was. I remember their crew, called the Finchley Boys. They grabbed one of their own roadies and completely gaffer taped him to the legs of the stage! A tough bunch. The Stranglers were incredible, though. I loved the bass sound of Jean-Jaques Burnel, and of course his playing was stellar.

Tonight, though, it was just us, and we knew this would be a great night. We had another gig at the end of the month in London, at the Music Machine in Camden, which we were well prepared for, and it was well attended. We were on with Bruce Woolley. This was a special night, because The Pack were on before us, and this was to be the first time I'd been on the same stage as Kirk Brandon, my great, great mate, although not together. The Pack were fantastic.

In June we played at the Factory, the Russell Club, in Manchester. I loved playing in Manchester. Next, we were off to Birmingham and Barbarella's, but I can barely remember the show.

It was then back down to London, to the famous Marquee Club on Wardour Street, where we were headlining. It was a memorable gig for a couple of reasons. We went onstage and it started well; we had the crowd in our back pocket as we fired on through the set. A crowd of skinheads were jostling about in the centre and something was going down at the front. They started spitting. Jim took umbrage and let them know if there was any more, we would down tools and go offstage! Of course, they kept on spitting. There was one big scary skinhead right at the front who was leading them on and trying to intimidate Jim. Jim picked up his microphone stand and whacked the guy over the head, who fell to the floor, muttering, 'What'd you do that for?' We marched offstage and sat in the dressing room for 20 minutes or so. The guy was carried out, and we finished our set.

Next we were playing Nottingham University. Everybody must go to Nottingham at least once. The castle is magnificent and you must visit the pub called Ye Olde Trip to Jerusalem. Nottingham audiences are great, and our show was not to disappoint. Our following gig on this dartboard tour, was in Wolverhampton, the home of Slade, and Wolverhampton Wanderers (Robert Plant's football team).

It was now 7 July, and we were back in London at the Nashville Rooms. I had played there before with the Subs. I remember Gary Numan, my old support act, came to see us. We were invited to go along to the Studios at Shepperton to participate in handclaps on his first album. Gary wanted to produce Simple Minds later on, but unfortunately it didn't happen. Nashville was great that night. All the usual record company people were there and our publishers at EMI too. On 12 July we drove to Chesterfield – a small gig, but equally enjoyable. The 13th was the Grey Topper, in Jacksdale, Nottinghamshire. Back and forth, and up and down the country – who bloody booked this tour?

In July we were in Derby and then Blackpool, where the Norbreck Castle Hotel has a huge ballroom. A great audience showed us their appreciation and we got a free stick of rock that night too. The downside of was the threatened stabbing of one of our roadies, big Alan McKinstrey. Some yobs had taken a dislike to his face and wanted to rearrange it. We were in the dressing room and oblivious. Big Al was quite shaken by what had happened but pulled himself together and soldiered on regardless, face still the same. We rolled on to Dudley the next day and found out that the gig had been cancelled. A day off! So, we bought Do-Dos from a chemist, an over-the-counter remedy for coughs and breathlessness that has an amphetamine-like action. We took a few tablets each and went to a film. Fuck me … my heart was beating like a fully wound-up toy drummer. I felt like marching on to Bremerhaven.

On the 24th we went back to the Marquee in London for round two. All fine, a superb audience and no spitting this time! I loved just being in London, it was beginning to feel like a second home. I remember a while back – I think in 1976 – I'd gone to London by train with my apprentice painter mate Jimmy Neilson, to look for a flat and a job for both of us. When we arrived, we bought a newspaper to look for rental flats. We traipsed about the streets, getting on and off the Tube and buses. Jimmy had a carry-out of beer and vodka, and got steadily pissed. We went for a burger in an attempt to sober him up. In Belsize Park, we headed to an address on our list for a rental. We were greeted by a stern landlady, who barked off the rules to us and really put us off. Although the area and the accommodation was adequate, we both looked at each other and blurted out, 'Fuck that.'

On to the Limit Club in Sheffield on 26 July. Now this gig was special. There were a few bands that we got to know and some that we liked. One we did like was the Human League – before they changed into a money-making machine. They had a guy with red hair playing the Revox two track; what a stroke of genius. Martyn Ware and the other bloke, Ian Craig Marsh, then teamed up with my old pal Glenn Gregory to form Heaven 17, a name nicked from the Milk Bar in *Clockwork Orange*. Sheffield also had Def Leppard, who we would see on quite a number of occasions. In fact, they later lived near Jim, Charlie and Bono in Killiney, Dublin. The Limit Club and its marvellous promotions team had the place packed for us. It was wall to wall Yorkshire people. It was one of the best clubs around at that time. Our show went really well that night.

I was regularly sent out front by the band after the gig to invite some ladies to meet the band. Being the oldest and a bit of a looker (I am too humble), I was always given this job. I am not completely sure, but I think this was the night that Mick met Hannah (they later married) and her gig pal Carole. Mick and I shared a room, and I can remember waking up in the morning with Hannah jumping up and down on my bed. She was a bit of a wild card then. Carole was a bit of a goth and was friends with Adam Ant at the time. We nicknamed her 'the Deid Yin' (the Dead One), due to her deathly white make-up and black eyes.

The next day we were off to play Eric's in Liverpool. Hannah and Carole followed us. It was a raucous night. I loved every minute and wished we could have stayed longer. Off we went in the morning to the Grey Topper, oh the heights! And then on to the Fforde Grene Hotel in Leeds. We had played this place earlier in the year before the Magazine tour. I remember having some of our friends come back to the hotel with us for an after-show bash. The hotel was in the centre of Leeds and quite plush. The night manager was very odd. We were ordering drinks and he was saying 'No, we don't have that', 'Let me see … no we don't have that either.' Someone asked for a vodka and Coke, and – joy of joy – the man lit up. 'Oh yes … we do have that … the reason I know we have Coke is that I like Coke myself, you see.' The band ended up ignoring him and going behind the bar to help themselves. The things you do when you are young!

We then headed back to smoggy old London Town, to the Music Machine, and then drove back to bonnie Scotland to play at the George Theatre in Edinburgh on 2 August. We were doing more miles than the Navy – which, incidentally, I nearly joined in 1972, after passing my medical (cough)! They told me I would be going down to Portsmouth to join up with more recruits, and then he asked me if I had any hobbies. I said I'm learning guitar and he stopped me, mid-sentence: 'Oh you won't have time to play guitar in the Navy, but we do have some of the finest brass bands in the forces!' Thank God I hadn't put pen to paper yet. I thought fuck that and left quickly.

Back down south we went to the Kirklevington Country Club for the next gig. Another success, a lovely venue and we were still pulling the crowds. The next gig was at the Rock Garden in Middlesbrough, on 4 August. It was a depressing place, and this venue was notorious for being full of hard bar stewards. The stage was about 2.5 m (8 feet) off the floor and was partially caged, like an old Blues Brothers gig. The crowd looked mean. To be fair we were ripped out of our minds, and we couldn't tell or give a fuck where we were. We just wanted to play.

After we left Middlesbrough, we had a couple of days to get down to the Marquee London again for our gig on the 7th. This was our best show yet. Something about playing on that stage drew out the best in the musicians. I remember Brian and I going to Golden Square near Soho to buy a pair of boxing boots from Lonsdale's. They were perfect for him on the drums, plus they could double as odour eaters. There was a crowd of people queuing up for Brian's autograph. (Funny thing about Brian, he did get mistaken for Bryan Adams once when he was on duty with Propaganda, and he signed for a few people … true!) Brian used to take my guitar up to the desk at any airport we were flying from and tell them, 'This is Buddy Holly's first guitar, could you please put it somewhere safe in the cabin.' – and they did. Elvis's guitar was another one he would use … genius!

The next day we were going to the BBC Paris Theatre in Regent Street for a live radio show with the Pretenders. This was the first time Jim met Chrissie. The Pretenders were fantastic; this was the original band with Martin Chambers, Pete Farndon, James Honeyman-Scott and Chrissie Hynde. Our soundman, Frank Gallagher, nicknamed the lead guitar player James Honeymoon-Suite. Sadly, both Pete and James are no longer with us.

Real to Real Cacophony

In August we drove to the wilds of Monmouthshire and set up camp at the Old Mill to get prepared for our second album *Real to Real Cacophony* at Rockfield Studios. We had the inimitable producer John Leckie at the helm. We barely had any songs or ideas and had to come up with the goods quick style!

The Old Mill was a huge old farmhouse about a mile or so along the road from Rockfield Studios. Our gear was set up in the big rehearsal room on the ground floor. In the days before our official recording started, we hammered out some ideas. The slate wasn't totally clean, and some great musical ideas were slowly being built. As usual Jim would record everything on his trusty ghetto blaster. During our downtime we would go into Monmouth and have a wee sherbet in the local pub. I made a friend and invited her to the rehearsal room and she ended up staying for the next few days. In the recording studio were also the wonderful Teardrop Explodes. They were staying up at Little Anchor Hill.

One early summer evening, the band appeared at our door, and we had a great amount of liquid madness and smokey. I went upstairs with my special friend, and her friend. Brian was conned into taking a friend upstairs too as a decoy for me. Suddenly there was an outrageous hullabaloo of marching feet coming upstairs to catch us out. Big Gary Dwyer from the band battered down Brian's door, and he and the woman were soaked and pelted with flour and food and whatever else. Brian just smiled and took the abuse. I escaped through the skylight window with the woman, both of us naked. The horde then forced the skylight. Mick MacNeil was at the front of the band of assailants, brandishing a fire extinguisher, firing away at our skinny unprotected bodies. I tried to push the skylight shut and managed to smash the window and cut open my arm. I still have the scar.

In the next couple of days, Teardrop Explodes finished their recordings and headed back to Liverpool. We moved into their accommodation at Little Anchor Hill. The house was up a farm track across from the main Studio block. When we entered the house, we were greeted with a wee present from the Teardrops. The kitchen looked totally empty, but, when we looked up, all the chairs that belonged around the kitchen table and a small sofa and kitchen cabinet had all been expertly gaffer taped to the ceiling. I went into my designated bedroom, and someone was asleep in the bed, obviously after a good skelp at the drink. It was none other than the Welsh lead singer Andy Fairweather Low of Amen Corner ('If Paradise is Half as Nice') fame! He looked a bit sheepish, got up and left quietly.

We eventually moved back into the Coach House Studio for recording, and began to write a bunch of completely new songs. Charlie had a chord sequence that was inspired by a Rolling Stones song, 'Citadel'. I had never heard it before, so I played a lot of root notes pertaining to the chords. This was the start of 'Changeling'. It needed a different angle. John Leckie told me that he was running off a cassette for me, and that he wanted me to go write a hit bass line. I took the cassette and went into the anteroom, played the track and heard in my head a complete bass line. I was away for around 10 minutes, and I was ready, so I went back into the control room and presented the bass line to John and the band. Everybody loved what I had come up with. Mick doubled my bass line with one of his synths (the Korg), and Brian played a great disco beat, one that he had been inspired by the future producer of 'Don't You (Forget About Me)', Keith Forsey. Keith, or 'Eyebrow McKenna' as we had named him, was the drummer for Donna Summer on her disco tracks. McGee was a huge fan of her stuff. Charlie then changed most of what he had done before and came up with fantastic guitar parts – not the riff as Kerr said in a documentary. Jim added his vocals, and the song was complete. We were incredibly quick at putting this together. I thrived on being able to come up with good ideas and quickly. Give me a basic rhythm or a few chords or a short piece of music, and the idea would come. I could easily transfer the ideas to my bass. That became my strength.

'Film Theme' was recorded with Brian McGee's drums set up in the corridor of the Coach House. John Leckie used this unique feature for a lot of the album; it created such a fine ambient sound for recording.

In the early part of our stay at Rockfield, Brian and I would go horse riding in the Forest of Dean. We arranged to go out riding with the guys from the Cockney Rejects. One of them hadn't fastened the girth, the belt that holds the saddle in place, and as he mounted the horse, the saddle slipped right under the horse, leaving him clinging on for dear life. Brian got whacked in the face with a trailing branch. It nearly knocked him good-looking!

We must have been about one week or so in the Coach House Studio when we heard of visitors arriving at the Courtyard Studio. It was Iggy Pop, and he had James Williamson of the Stooges with him. James was producing Iggy's *Soldier* album. Iggy had also brought a friend with him: David Bowie. I was shopping for supplies in Monmouth when Iggy's entourage arrived. I went into our studio where Jim Kerr was sitting, and he told me that Bowie was in the other studio with Iggy. Then he asked me if I would go up and ask Bowie to maybe play some saxophone on a track or something.

I said OK, I'll do that. No problem. I was just about to walk out when I asked Jim if I should wear my stage gear and whacky eye make-up I used for live shows. He said that's a good idea. So, I did. I walked up the path to the door of the Courtyard Studio and entered the small porch area. To my right was the control room, and to my left was the games room. This had a safety glass panel in the door, and I saw that somebody was in there. I opened the door and was confronted by two smiling gentlemen sitting cross-legged on the table tennis table. One faced me and the other who had his back to me looked over his shoulder. It was David and Iggy. I introduced myself and told them we were working in the other studio. David, who faced me, asked, 'Do you sing?' I said yes and told him I did backing vocals with our band. He said, 'Great, we need a big chorus for this song that Jim (Iggy) is recording.' I said, 'Should I get our singer?' And David smiled and said 'Yes.' So, I went quickly down the path to get Jim Kerr.

We went back up the path to the studio and went into the recording room and met up with Iggy's band, who were ready to make up the chorus line. The chorus personnel were Glen Matlock (Sex Pistols), Barry Andrews (XTC), Patti Palladin (US punk singer and musician with Johnny Thunders), Steve New (Rich Kids), Ivan Kral (Patti Smith), Jim Kerr, David Bowie and myself. The song was 'Play it Safe', and David was directing the whole thing and dancing away while recording and giving us lines to sing. He was battering into me with his hips and almost knocking me out of the circle – not because I was shit, you'll understand, but because he, at that time, was the Thin White Duke. After we recorded the chorus, Iggy put down his lead vocals. The next morning, I sat for hours with Iggy in the control room as he recorded more vocals. He asked me for my opinion after every line he sang. Brilliant.

It was the night of the wrap party for Iggy and the band. They were staying at the Old Mill. I was with John Leckie in his little MG. We were driving up the road to the Little Anchor Hill to get the hash we had stashed. John crashed the car halfway up the driveway. No real damage, I am glad to say, but we missed a great wizard wheeze at the Old Mill car park. The head of A & R from Arista had driven up to Rockfield and arrived in a blaze of glory sporting his brand-new car. He was quite aloof. He would do edits of our singles in his office and present them to us. We would tell him to fuck off, or possibly our manager would; we weren't fans. Some people, who shall not be named, attacked his new car: they opened the doors and lobbed in boxes of cornflakes, bags of flour, sugar, a family-sized bottle of washing-up liquid, washing powder and one of the bandits threw a couple of dozen eggs as well. Now, remember it was the end of June when this happened, and the weather was warm, so the car the next morning was cooking. You can take the boys out of Glasgow, but you can't take Glasgow out of the boys.

We blamed our engineer, Pat Moran, for the wanton destruction, but Charles Levison, managing director of Arista , was convinced that it was me. As you know, I was elsewhere at the time, but I would have been proud to be part of the mayhem. We carried on for another couple of weeks recording and mixing the album, and as a nice parting gesture Brian McGee, who was driving our blue Bedford Minibus, rolled down the driver's window and smashed an egg on the back of one of the owner's daughters' heads as we left. Oh, how we laughed …

Simple Minds were having a great time musically at this time and we felt that we were a crack unit of friends. Jim and I put what you might mildy call whacky vocals on the track 'Veldt'! I had recorded the bass and the piano part as well. Imagine the faces of the oligarchs at Arista when they heard this fantastic toe tapper! I thought that the track 'Factory' was a standout on the album and 'Changeling', 'Scar', and 'Film Theme' were genius. 'Premonition' became a truly loved live performance track. It would be almost a year before we would return to Rockfield Studios, to do it all again.

Real to Real Cacophony Tour

With the album *Real to Real Cacophony* in the bag, we were ready to venture further afield, way across the water that lay between us, and into Germany. This would be our first performance in mainland Europe. We boarded the ferry from Harwich, bound for Hamburg on an overnight sailing, and had our very own cabins. Probably to keep us out of trouble! We met in the bar and proceeded to get pissed. We ate some of the food on offer, black bread and sauerkraut. Brian McGee remarked that after he had a shit that night, it resembled a Doberman Pinscher's, all brown and black. It coined the phrase '*Deutsche Braun Schwarze Kech*' which meant, to us, German brown, black shit. Please excuse us, we were young and daft!

In the morning we left the ship and went outside to set our eyes on Hamburg for the very first time. It looked incredible. The first gig was the Fabrik, a disused factory (the German word means *factory*). Having lived and worked in Spain for five months, I had picked up quite a bit of Spanish, and now that I was in Germany, I tried to pick up a bit of the local language as well. My first German phrase was: '*Wo ist die toilette, bitte?*' We played a blinder in Fabrik. Billy Wharton did the sound for us, and David Henderson assisted Billy and Jaine Henderson with the lights. The two Dougies were our crew, Wee Dougie Wragg and Big Dougie Cowan. We had bought a 3,000-watt PA system with our advance money and were later wise enough to rent it out when we weren't playing. A couple of bands who hired it from us were the Human League and Spandau Ballet.

Next day we went to Berlin. Good old Berlin. Checkpoint Charlie, Unter den Linden, Küfürstendamm, Kempinski's, Der Reichstag, und die Mauer – or you may know it as the Wall. A beautiful city with a dark past. We, of course, made for all the sights: a few hundred metres to the left were wooden lookout posts with steps up to the platform at the top. We could see right across Niemandsland, or no man's land, a troughed area strewn with hidden land mines. A gift from the Soviets who patrolled the wall. We could see a huge radio communications mast that looked like a spike skewering a football. We called it the Berlin Ball.

We were to play on Kant Straße at the Kant-Kino the following night. After our bout of tourism, we ate at a local restaurant and later went out to a club. We went to the bar, and there, in front of us, was a glass case in the shape of a table. It had lizards in it, real lizards. Of course, Brian McGee, the Johnny Morris of the band, tried to take one out, but he never managed. The barman asked Brian what he would like. 'A dry martini,' he replied and within a few minutes the barman returned with three dry martinis. Brian complained that he only wanted one, but the barman said you asked for three! *Boom, boom! Get it?* Of course, the German word for three is *drei*. At the Kant-Kino gig there was a healthy crowd waiting for us. Having only played our first gig in Hamburg a couple of nights ago, we began to work out the way the audience treated newcomers at concerts. After every song there would be an awkward silence. All we could hear was the odd cough and the rattling of sweetie papers. We thought that we had given our all and we carried on till the end of our set. We walked off to the sound of squeaky floorboards, and couldn't understand this odd response. When we reached the dressing room, there was a huge sound coming from the audience in the auditorium. They were chanting *Zugabe, Zugabe, Zugabe …* at the top of their collective voices. This meant encore … so apparently they had loved our set. We went back onstage for an encore, and after that they cheered again, and again. Reassuring us that we were a cool beat combo!

The following day we left Berlin, through the barriers and customs, entering into East Germany, for the transit route though occupied West Germany to occupied East Germany and, finally, onto West Germany. We passed Soviet troops with furry fruit pastel hats on, mere boys in uniform amid the tanks and missiles, which looked threatening and aggressive to the max. We tried stopping at a shop to get some food, only to find shelves bare apart from cheese and a small amount of bread. We re-entered West Germany via checkpoints again and headed for Hannover for a first-time gig at the Rotation Club. As we drove along, slightly lost, we saw a young chubby boy walking along near us. We stopped, rolled down the window and I said, 'Excuse me, I'm a rockstar, can you tell me where the gig is?' The band all laughed. McGee shouted something like 'Wee fatty doesn't speak English!' And the boy piped up,

'I am English … ha ha,' so, with our gas at a peep, we brought him into the van and he took us to the gig.

The gig was huge. The audience was playing games again, and they went through the ritual of making us think we were shite. I think we played there the next night at the behest of Dutch beat combo Golden Earring. On 14 October we were back in Hamburg for a second stint at Fabrik. It got better and better. Word was spreading, and our audiences began to swell. We certainly left our mark in Hamburg.

In the morning we were up early to travel to Bremen, where the show was at the Aladin Music Hall. Now this gig was famous for the slap back echo that you could hear if you clapped your hands: it would repeat tenfold, like a fast echo. It was like an old-time burlesque hall, with a circus-like appearance. We set up and did the soundcheck, which was traditionally 'The Sash My Father Wore' – which pleased me, but the rest of them just liked the tune. During this gig wee Dougie Wragg, our roadie, crawled inside a bass bin during the show and fell asleep. At the end of the set, it was the usual silence. This time we thought we weren't getting an encore, and the roadies were complaining, saying: 'Who won the war anyway?', which was a tad out of order. But just like the previous time, the old *Zugabe* started to ring out in our ears, and we went back on, delighted.

Dougie Wragg, Simple Minds roadie

Back at the hotel we got pissed, stoned, fed and sent off to bed. The next morning was cold. We boarded our luxury 12-seater van and made our way to Nürnberg, the darkest of all places. I remember meeting a Scottish guy, a 'Willie, I know ye' familiar bastard, who was a wee bit too cocky for my liking. He turned out to be a bit of a bully, trying to intimidate us, but after our show he was left in our wake; we hoped we would never see him again.

The next day were off to play in Brussels, at Auderghem Canotier. Brussels is now a stronghold for Simple Minds, and this was our first gig there. It laid the foundations for many a return performance. Brian McGee drove us everywhere and we never really thanked him for it. I am sure Brian didn't trust anyone else, having seen the other band members' driving skills. Jim drove like a pensioner; Mick would drive past and raise his middle finger. Charlie nearly gave me and Pete Walsh a heart attack as he drove through winding country roads, bending down to change cassette tapes at breakneck speed. Me, I wasn't any great shakes either. How I passed a car and a motorbike test, I'll never know. Brian's last driving day in Europe turned out to be a nightmare. He had scraped the side of our van, and things escalated a wee bit! He then declared that he wasn't going to play the gig. Eddie Cairns suggested we ignored him, and he eventually played. Brian had a wee greet, and he received in honour the nickname Greety McGee.

Old Grey Whistle Test **New York**

On 22 October we were leaving for America. Our wonderful management had managed to swing it for us to appear onstage at a couple of clubs over there in the Big Apple. This was a personal dream of mine. We were crossing the pond for the first time. We played at Hurrah in Manhattan for the *Old Grey Whistle Test* for the BBC. Hurrah was a nightclub where David Bowie had just finished his video for 'Fashion'. Jim, Charlie and I did an interview on Broadway with the iconic 'Whispering Bob' Harris. When asked by the Whispering one what we had been up to, I rambled on about gigs in Tiffany's and other exciting stuff. I had to pinch myself at being in New York. The Police had filmed the day before at Cape Canaveral in Florida, banging sticks off space rockets and the like. It was *Whistle Test* gold.

Once we got onstage, we were ready, though we only played a limited set. Jim, with his bowl haircut danced all bendy leggy, while Mick, stoned as a hippy, tinkled the ivories for all he was worth. Charlie looked cool dancing over his pedal board to the rhythm of Brian McGee bashing away on his drums at the back of the stage. I do remember there were cheers for 'Garden of Hate'. It felt surreal. There is great footage of the Hurrah show and if you watch it, you can see me smiling down at someone in the audience at the front of the stage. It was none other than the legend James 'Iggy Pop' Osterberg. Blondie was also in the audience, watching, and a few more of the elite Manhattan set too. New York is that kind of place. You never know who will turn up at your shows!

The following night, we played at a gig called Trax, just along from where, by the end of the following year, John Lennon would be shot and killed. In Trax that night there were lots of women, and I mean *a lot*. We hadn't realised how well known we were becoming! Later we found out that the girls were courtesy of the record company, hired to swoon and cheer at us all through the set.

In the short time that we were there, we learned not to look up at the buildings so obviously: it was a sure sign that you were a tourist, and that could make you a target for muggers. Our big band boffin, Dougie Cowan, was so freaked out by all the sirens and what sounded like gunshots going off, he never came out of his room to go out for a wander at nighttime, not even for food. The hotel was just across the road from the Metropole, or the Met.

Now that we had tasted the United States, the band were well up for more. The diners looked as though they were straight out of a film, and I loved the endless supply of coffee. Irish pubs were everywhere, but no Scottish bars! We loved the camera shops, which had loads of gadgets too, like Walkmans and video cameras. I went for a walkabout with Charlie, Brian and Mick. Jim stayed in the hotel, writing Brian's part for 'Garden of Hate'. On our last night we went for a band meal, paid for by Bruce, our manager, in a Japanese restaurant. The food was marvelous and the sake dangerous. As we went to leave, a big man came out angrily and confronted Bruce, asking if we liked the food. Then he reminded Bruce that we hadn't tipped. We soon learned that tipping was expected! At the Iroquois Hotel we met up with Iggy again, and for a bunch of young boys this whole jaunt had seemed like a dream.

When I returned back home to Glasgow, I went to Brian's pad for a wee smoke of the peace pipe and a Chinese takeaway. In our normal surroundings, our recent New York Trip seemed like a dream. We looked at each other and blurted out, 'Did that really happen?'

* * *

Our next gigs were to be in Europe once more, this time Sweden, starting off in Errol's in Gothenburg and followed by the famous Music Palais in Stockholm. I particularly remember the journey and especially the beautiful coloured houses, which I felt really represented Scandinavia. Apparently, the idea behind the bright colours was to try and keep spirits up during the long dark winter. Six months of darkness every year – the Scandinavians are hardy folk; all power to them.

We had a bit of a shock when we went into a café and ordered coffee. The bill for each coffee was £10. We discovered that the price of a pint of beer was rather high too. We were on 'two sticks and a balloon, and a blaw at a rag man's trumpet' in terms of wages then. The night at the Music Palais was fantastic. I never knew there could be so many beautiful people in one place. At a gig in Aarhus at Musikteatret, we first drank Carlsberg Elephant Beer. Which, over there, had hallucinogenic traits. We couldn't get enough of it. There were a few sore heads following the after-show bash. Our *rock and roll, one long weekend* lifestyle was hardening us, so hangovers no longer felt anywhere near as bad as they once had.

Home Turf Again: University Tour

The show we did recently in New York had been recorded, so we had to record overdubs. Mick was at Brian Young's CaVa Studios to sort out his parts for a week before we could continue, so on the agenda was rehearsals, which were held upstairs in the attic at the Edinburgh Odeon on Lothian Road. We rehearsed every day.

The next gig was at Stirling University. We had a friend of Bruce's come along to the show to work with us on this one. I think his name was Eddie. There were bottles of red wine set out for us in amongst the rest of the gargle. I was given a quick lesson by Eddie on the downside of red wine. He insisted there was too much formaldehyde in red, and that it was far better to drink white wine. For ages after that, I never drank it. (I was later told that a good red wine was far superior, while dining with management team Bruce Findlay and Robert White, at a hotel in Seattle, Washington.) After the show, I met the great Mick Ronson at the bar. We became good friends.

I moved out to Stirlingshire in 1998, and met one of the parents from the primary school that my kids went to; he had been to that show in Stirling all those years ago. It was his first gig. His name was Derek too, and he hated the name, so he was known as Der. He was a coach painter, and I'd been a painter too. I wasn't doing much in music at that time, so we joined forces and formed a painting company. We racked our brains for a suitable name for the company and we came up with Coppola-Kantz. We put adverts in the *Stirling Observer* and work started to come in. It wasn't till later that some people sussed the name. I remember people asking about decoration of a house or flat, and 'What are you going to do, paint it yourself?' 'No, I'll just get a couple a cunts in to paint it.'

This was mainly a university tour, and it was great to be doing these sorts of venues. We always went down well in Aberdeen, and this was no different; we had a great turnout. Forbes country, what did you expect? We were going home the next day for a gig at the Queen Margaret Union, in Glasgow's West End. Good old Glasgow, you never let us down. Again, this gig was rammed. Everyone and their granny were there that night. This was the forerunner for our Tiffany's gig.

Would 1979 ever end? I get tired just thinking about all the miles we travelled (never mind actually travelling those miles) – but whenever we had a day off, we were usually champing at the bit to get in the bus and go again, such is the narcotic effect of the music business. Off we go next to St Andrews University. This was a step up from our last visit to St Andrews: the hall we played in was large, stunning, and welcoming. We managed to fill it for our show. The students were good fun and very appreciative. We were looked after well, staying in a lovely B & B in town. Richard Jobson of the Skids was there with us for this gig. Now St Andrews is not Las Vegas, let's establish that. There are no late-night kebab shops or pizza shops open after hours, so food was scarce here in the wee small hours. We all assembled in one of our rooms and we hatched a cunning plan. It was Saturday night, and we were sure there would be Sunday lunch prepared in the kitchens for tomorrow's hungry guests. With Jobson leading the way, we crept down the stairs to the kitchen and tiptoed in for a quick look. In the fridge was a cooked chicken, a big one at that. It managed to fly out of the kitchen to be shared by a horde of hungry Scotsmen. We turned up for breakfast, and the man in charge knew who had taken the bird from the kitchen but had no proof. I wish I could send some money to him now for it, but that bird has flown.

It was 19 November and Edinburgh's finest welcomed us back. Tiffany's in Edinburgh it was, and we were ready to serve up good music. 'Life In a Day' went down a treat as did 'Pleasantly Disturbed'. During our regular meetings with Bruce in Edinburgh he would often invite all the great and the good from Auld Reekie, and he would regale them with stories, holding court like only he could.

A gig at Newcastle University was a bit of a downer, to say the least. We were onstage playing, looking cool and getting down when a fight broke out between us – mid-song through 'Wasteland', I think – and some arseholes in the audience. We left the stage, and the perpetrators were shown the door. After 15 minutes or so we went back on for the remainder of the set. A few days later one of the A & R men from Arista came in to see us at a later gig and remarked that it was a great gig in Newcastle. Which just showed us he hadn't been there. What a mullet-haired twat he was. This was a nail firmly hammered into the Arista/Simple Minds coffin.

It was Charlie's birthday on 27 November, and we were playing at the Music Hall in Shrewsbury. Colchester next. Wales again, and the Troubadour in Port Talbot. Back in Liverpool again, back at Eric's, and by 1 December we're at the Student Union at Manchester Poly. Peter Hook (Joy Division, New Order) was at this one. We got on alright as bass brothers. Hooky is one of the earliest influences on me as a bass player. The next day, we head back again to the Fforde Grene.

Off to the University of East Anglia and a gig in Norwich. Next, the Limit in Sheffield. This time we saw Phil Oakey, the Human League's man at the front. The Limit never let us down.

It was getting near Christmas and our next gig was at North Staffs Polytechnic, Stafford. After checking into our hotel which was close to the gig, we took a walk into the beautiful town of Stafford. It was a chilly, frosty night and the town was full of Christmas lights; it looked magical.

In the morning we headed to Robin Hood country. We played at the Sandpiper in Nottingham. Exeter was beckoning us for the next gig. It was going to be a long drive, so there was not a lot of partying for us that night. We turned up early in the afternoon at the University of Exeter. Exeter has beautiful Tudor buildings dotted around the center.

Great shops too. It reminded me of Bath. A typical University gig full of beautiful students. Seemed a lot different from my college days. I went to Langside College in Glasgow and you may remember me mentioning that I played a gig booked, and Ian Reekie brought along a very young Jim Kerr to see my show at the College.

The Keele show had a memorable moment with a great picture of us with a load of students holding a poster and one guy had his bare arse out. Our roadie Eddie Cairns swears we went home after this, but he says he may just have forgotten. I'm not sure we went home because we definitely played the Marquee, London on 13–14 December. A very successful couple of gigs this time.

Eddie Cairns, Simple Minds driver and roadie, RIP

The last gig of 1979 was at Glasgow Technical College. I know this was a good night, as it was Hogmanay. The show started earlier than usual so people could make it home to welcome in the New Year together. What a year we had had: two albums and a plethora of tours and gigs in the UK, America and mainland Europe.

Bigger Things to Come

Bigger things were about to happen for Simple Minds. The work on the third album *Empires and Dance* was planned to commence on my birthday in June, but we started 1980 with yet more gigs.

On 7 January we were to play Tiffany's in Glasgow. I used to go to a club every Monday night, Smokey Joes in Tiffany's. I met and chatted with Frankie Miller there a few times. Mick MacNeil worked with Frankie later in his career. The only band I remember from Monday nights was called Long Vehicle; they were a great band although the name stank. Names mean nothing really. I mean, look at Simple Minds, an awful name; it was lucky the Bowie connotations came to the fore, because once it had been established it didn't seem so bad.

In January 'Changeling' was released and it soon became a favourite of the top DJ in London at that time, a very young Rusty Egan. Rusty needed a hand with some recordings, so Mick MacNeil and I helped recording parts of bass and keyboards for some new Visage tracks. At the time, we were having a bit of an ongoing battle with our record company Arista. I don't think they agreed with our music and direction, and we could see the writing on the wall. We went to meet several Arista people from various departments at the restaurant Brown in Berkeley Square in Central London. It was a posh fish and chip shop and we had to scare away the seagulls so that we could hear ourselves talking. The purpose of the meeting was for the band and management to discuss the differences, to have it out face to face. We set about them in a very splintered way. I took on the art department, Charlie faced up to the A & R department, Jim, Bruce and Robert challenged the managing director. Brian and Mick had a go at anyone else who deserved a good talking to. When the dust settled, it was kind of clear that our time together was coming to an end. Things were so bad we even thought about disbanding the band, just to be released from the contract. We eventually cooled off, had food and drinks, then fucked off back to the Columbia hotel for a chinwag. During the armistice, a couple of us ordered piña coladas, which went down like a lead balloon with the managing director Charles Levison. He stood up and announced that only the band could order piña coladas and no one else! Our heroic manager, Bruce Findlay, stood up and roared: 'The piña coladas are on me!' So everyone ordered them.

The disagreements between us continued well into the end of the year but we carried on gigging. We started in London, headed to Paris (totally buzzing), back to Britain, off to Germany for quite a few gigs, then back to France.

We continued our European tour and made a first visit to Liège, Belgium, at Salle de la Chapelle on 12 March 1980. I'm knackered thinking about it! As most people involved in touring bands would know, at every gig there are riders. Riders are items required by the band for every show, i.e. technical equipment, food, drink and meals for the band and crew – and Smarties, but only the red ones.

On this tour we had requested steak and chips every day for the band, every day. Lo and behold, when we arrived at the venue, we were taken to a beautiful restaurant for our daily meal. It was especially well presented, and we ate our steak and chips heartily. We had a rule, a strict rule, that we would be ready at the gig at least one hour before stage time. The waiter took forever to bring us the bill, which in turn, made us late and we arrived about 15 minutes before showtime. We got into our stage clothes and put on our stage makeup, and we were ready. I turned to Jim and told him that I had a one in the chute. A problem, as there was no toilet backstage; the only toilets were at the back of the hall which by now was packed with at least a thousand excited fans. Jim comforted me with, 'It's only an hour-long show, you'll be fine!' The first song was 'Capital City', which we used as an opening number and which began with an atmospheric bass line, which had a break, then a slight pause before I carried on with the riff. I had gone into a cold sweat, as I was now at the 'touching cloth' stage! I pulled off my bass, handed it to Jim, dashed offstage to the dressing room, found a paper bag. I tossed the offending bag outside as far as I could. I went back onstage to find Jim singing that old refrain 'shitey, shitey' while swinging my bass around his head. Having no toilet paper made my arse akin to a Black Forest gateau.

Empires and Dance

It was now the time for our next album, *Empires and Dance*, to be written and recorded. Work officially started on my birthday, 22 June. We were already ahead of the game, having worked on tracks at soundchecks. We went back to the Old Mill at Rockfield in Wales. Our usual schedule for an album would be five weeks writing and rehearsing and five weeks in the studio, recording and mixing the album. Just as before, Jim sat on top of my amp with a notepad. There was time in our schedule to relax too. Jim walked into the TV room at the Old Mill as we were watching some programme or other and he asked us what we were watching. We told him, and he whipped out his trouser snake and pissed on the television. We fell into shrieks of laughter and hysterics, then composed ourselves. One of us, probably me, called the office of the studios to complain about the smell of piss coming from the TV. A couple of the owners came down to see us, sniffed the television, and agreed that it did reek of piss and replaced it. Unbelievable behaviour, not proud of it now.

Any downtime Brian McGee and I had at Rockfield we would, as before, go horse riding through the Forest of Dean, or we would fuck around in the land surrounding the place. I bought an inflatable dinghy from a petrol station in Hereford for about fourpence ha'penny. I took my girlfriend for a leisurely cruise in it on the calm waters of the river at the back of the Mill. Calm, my arse! It was treacherous, fast-moving, white-water rafting madness. We careered into an overhanging branch and within about 10 seconds the dinghy had capsized, and we instinctively grabbed hold of the branch. We were being pounded by the rushing water. I managed to get a foothold below us and pulled the branch as hard as I could, and she managed to get her feet on the rocks below. We slowly pulled ourselves to the bank, which was stupidly steep, and we scrambled up to the dry ground above. Well scary. Paula Yates wrote a great piece about our mishap in one of the Sunday supplements, making me out to be a hero. Actually, I was a bit of a twat for buying the flimsy deathtrap in the first place.

Our songwriting was coming on strong now. The sessions at the Old Mill helped us ease into the studio and the album had quite an easy birth. 'This Fear of Gods' helped me be more creative on the old Fender Precision Fretless bass. What an epic track. On 'Today I Died Again' I had worked out my parts, and was reasonably happy with what I was playing, but then the genius who was John Leckie came over to me and said that I should try to bend some of the notes up to the key, rather than just play them straight. I gladly took his advice; he was right. 'Celebrate', another fretless song, was inspired by Eddy Grant. Brian really nailed the drum part for that song. If you listen carefully, you can hear – just before the first chorus 'we can live' comes in – Brian's voice shouting out 'get it up ye'. 'Constantinople Line' was reminiscent of our adventures on the transit route through East Germany into Berlin and the West. Again, Brian and I, the Rhythm Brothers, worked out an intricate drum and bass pattern. We were starting to be a little more eccentric in our

Simple Minds

Brian McGee and Derek, the Rythm Brothers

approach. Aye, yer auld arse! 'Capital City' was perfect. Charlie and Mick nailed this song, and the idiosyncratic performance from Jim was on the money.

Later we used 'Capital City' as our first song in one of our gigs in Canada, the Montreal Canada at Le Spectrum. Our intro tape had just stopped, and I was to come in with the bass pulse to start the song. We had our backs to the audience; the tension was building, and I took my time as the audience waited for the sound. Cheeky Brian McGee shouted to me: 'Hurry up, ya cunt,' and threw his drumstick at my guitar, which sounded out with a big clang, a veritable tuneless explosion. The band were in stitches.

'I Travel' was a real adventure of sound. Mick's incredible starting sequence enthralled audiences around the world. The huge slaps you hear on the recording were made by all the band, John Leckie and the girlfriends who were there, standing around the table tennis room and slapping down as hard as we all could, on the table. Travel round, I travel round.

I think the next song, 'Thirty Frames a Second', is one of my favourite bass lines. When mixed in with the drums, it sounds like conga drums to me, but then I am totally mad. The backwards drums are astounding, and Mick's deep keyboard parts incredible, and there are fantastic guitar parts from Charlie. The cackle is proper witchcraft. I love the way the song ends on the record with a segue into a film projector as the tape ends. 'Room' is the next song in line. We wrote this at the BBC Studios in Delaware Road, Maida Vale, London. The producer that day was Dale Griffin, aka Buffin from Mott the Hoople. We had just finished recording all the songs that we thought we could do in the time allotted. Buffin asked us if we had any more tracks that we would like to do, as there was five minutes left of the session. So, Jim, Charlie, Mick, Brian and I went back into the recording room and quickly wrote 'Room', managing to record it there and then. It hardly varies from the track that you hear on *Empires and Dance*. The penultimate track was 'Twist/Run/Repulsion', dedicated to Jim's French girlfriend, Catherine of 'Colours Fly' fame .

I had begun to write on my bass. I just looked at the finger board and imagined that I was writing letters on the bass guitar. 'Thirty Frames a Second' was a Y. 'Twist/Run/Repulsion' was a series of Xs and so on and on. That is how the bass line was developed and written. It wasn't played live, as it wasn't deemed a toe-tapper, although it did go down well. One of the last songs on the album was the wonderful 'Kant-Kino', an homage to the beautiful little cinema in Kant Straße, Berlin. On one of our early visits, I met a lass called Dagmar Pfaff, and she took me to her home in Berlin. She knew the guys from Ultravox and was a great music fan. The band nicknamed her my wife way back then. I remember leaving Berlin and being ridiculed by the band to the sound of 'Heroes' by David Bowie. Next time we went back to Berlin, on the same tour, I was sharing with Mick. I met Dagmar on arrival and then I left to go to the shops for something. On my return, the door was locked, so I banged on the door and Mick answered, but he didn't let me in. I worked out straightaway what was happening, the rascal.

The album was finished and would soon be in the hands of the Arista management team, who were reluctant to release it. We get ready for the Peter Gabriel tour of mainland Europe.

Peter Gabriel Tour

There seems to be some confusion about when this wonderful tour with Peter Gabriel actually started. I will go with the recollection of our trusted driver, guide, confidant, protector and big giant spider head, Eddie Cairns. We started the tour at the Audimax in Hamburg, Germany, on 1 September 1980. We were fans of Peter, and we couldn't believe that we would be with him for six weeks or so. Peter is a lovely man, of immense talent.

We had to try our best to win the Genesis audience over. Sometimes we would get a great response, but mostly it could be anything from mild applause to completely hostile. We played at Kuppelsaal, Hannover. This was one of our usual haunts. Peter's road crew were a lot of guys from Pink Floyd's camp. They were total professionals. On 4 September, we arrived in Berlin to play the Deutschland Halle. Ronnie Gurr was here with us. He was responsible for the fantastic photographs of the the band at the Berlin Wall. On 5 September we head to Phillipshalle, Düsseldorf. A town in Germany, where I lived for several months while in Propaganda and writing with Michael Mertens and Ralf Dörper. The following day we headed for Holland, to the Musiek Centrum in Utrecht and on 7 September we crossed another border into Belgium to play the Vorst National, Brussels.

Peter was great that night. He was great every night. The band entered the stage from different sides of the building. They wore black, custom-made boiler suits and carried big workmen's torches. The main

Derek on tour with Simple Minds, Germany

lights of the auditorium were turned off, and the band, with Peter, walked through the audience to complete their grand entrance to tumultuous applause. Just spine-tingling.

Next stop La Belle France. The tour took us to Paris where we played five nights at the Olympia Theatre, made famous by the Little Sparrow, Edith Piaf. We played every night from 9 September to the 13th. Peter cycled on his bike every day from the hotel to the venue, and no one would bat an eyelid. From Paris, we drove to Nantes, then headed back into Germany to play a show at the Stadthalle Offenbach, near Frankfurt. As usual we did our set, and I will say the Germans got us this time and were on our side. Off we went to our dressing room and settled down to relax. Peter Gabriel came in and asked me outside for a chat. John Giblin had been stuck in traffic in Frankfurt and was going to be late for the show, so Peter asked me to get ready and fill in for John: 'You know the songs by now, here's a Walkman, go and listen to the first few songs and we will go from there, I will cover you on the piano too.' So, I was all ready to go on when a flustered John Giblin came rushing in just in time. Drat.

Derek, on tour with Simple Minds in Paris

We had a few days off before our next port of call: Bordeaux. We tried out the local cuisine and, of course, the splendid wine. The very next day we went to Toulouse for two nights – though it was unusual for us to stay anywhere for two nights. Off to Italy in the morning, and Florence, home of ACF Fiorentina. I love Florence and the gig went well. Just as well; we knew that tomorrow we were being thrown to the lions at the Palasport in Genoa! We were expecting a bit of a rough reception – and we were not wrong. The audience were impatient to see Peter and the band, and we were pelted by bottles and cans. Brian McGee had cream cakes thrown at him and his drum kit was covered in delicious Italian desserts. Even so, I am pretty sure we were appreciated by the people of Genoa at the end of our set; to be fair, we were really fucking good!

Turin, 30 September, was a great gig. The people further up the boot are passionate about music, and they are very loud. They came in their droves to see the last Italian date of the tour. Complete madness, and we couldn't wait to go back.

On to pretty Avignon in France, and another big show, at the Parc des Expositions. The French certainly have a thing for the Scots, and we had a great time onstage. Then we headed to Spain for the last run of gigs and we were to play at the Pavelló Club Juventut Badalona, in Barcelona. I was back home to my beloved España. It brought back vivid memories of sunny days pissed as a fart, wandering about the streets, handing out leaflets to get bums on seats at the bar where I worked. We set off to Lloret de Mar with Eddie Cairns driving. We were so close that I had to go see my old bosses. John Giblin came along with us. We had become firm friends on that tour – so much so, that I would visit him in Holytown and meet his family at Christmas. Back to Lloret de Mar: we visited my old haunts, which luckily were still standing. We met up with my big Liverpool boss, Steve Watson. We stayed at the Corner Inn for a couple of hours, then we went to see my other old boss Mr Roger, who owned Paddy's Bar. I had been poached from the Corner Inn, where I was resident guitarist in the evenings and barman/manager during the day, to be part of a band who were booked for the season at Paddy's Bar. My wages tripled! A typical day at Paddy's was rehearsals from 2 p.m. till 6 p.m. every day except Sundays. And we would play from 10 p.m. till 4.30 a.m. every night of the week. There was an amiable jolly man called Double Dave, the bass player, named because he was a giant of a man, and Martin the drummer, both from Leeds. Double Dave was the bloke

I told you about earlier who couldn't play bass and sing at the same time, so I would fill in on bass.

One night on tour, Peter Gabriel asked us to don the costumes that lay in the cupboards backstage. They were huge heads and costumes reminiscent of *It's a Knockout* – or *Jeux Sans Frontiéres* for our European friends. At the opening notes of 'Games Without Frontiers', we walked onstage and danced around Peter and the band. It was moments like that that made the Gabriel Tour so special.

On that same tour, Brian McGee, the Simple Minds original – and most valued – drummer, was asked if he would like to play drums for the song 'Biko'. Steve Biko was a South African anti-apartheid activist who was arrested on 18 August at a roadblock in Port Elizabeth and jailed. On 11 September, he was found naked and shackled outside a hospital in Pretoria, about 1,200 km (740 miles) from Port Elizabeth. He died of a massive brain hemorrhage the next day. This was a very poignant song for Peter. Jerry Marotta, Peter's drummer, beckoned Brian McGee to come up to the drums and take over, so they kept the beat going and somehow managed to change over without as much as a lost tap of the drums. All was going well until the chorus when Brian whacked the cymbals to mark the change. Peter turned swiftly to see that Brian was now behind the kit. The problem was that, unbeknown to Brian, Peter Gabriel's third album had been recorded without cymbals, and there was Brian happily thrashing away to his heart's content.

We headed north, to Porto for the last night of the tour. It was sad to get to the end of the tour. I met a lovely woman after the show. She looked like Wonder Woman, with a silver tiara on her head, and she was a bit of a live wire too. I walked out of the gig, hand in hand, passing the road crew for both bands and by all the trucks. They were all cheering and whistling as we went on our way. I was sharing a room with Paul Wishart for the last time, and as I sat on the bed having a drink with Wonder Woman, all I could see was his baldy wee head peering out between the sheets staring at us.

Kelly Marie and the Disposable Camera

In the early days with Simple Minds, we would be booked for TV shows all over Europe. We were invited to perform at a music show in Munich, after the lovely Kelly Marie from bonnie Paisley, just outside of Glasgow. Kelly was a bit older than us and had just had a massive hit. She performed to the delight of the animated, disco-loving audience, and was a great sport. We sat around the table in the green room, having a few drinks and a good laugh with Kelly before leaving to get ready for our turn onstage in front of the cameras. We were, at that time, promoting *Real to Real Cacophony*, the second album. We left the studios and gathered in the foyer of the hotel. We were supposed to be heading to the restaurant for food and drink, but some of us wandered through doors and ended up partially clothed in the hotel swimming pool. I remember Charlie was feeling a bit down, possibly from a phone call home, or a fallout … so what to do?

After our sobering swim and frolics we returned to one of the rooms and carried on with the party, smoking and drinking. At this time one of us had a disposable camera – Mick, I think. The hilarity exploded into a mad impromptu party. Jim surprised us all as he came out of the bathroom, totally bollock naked, with a towel over his head and wearing a pair of Wellington boots, for a laugh. After that everyone started to act outrageous. When Mick got home, he left the camera in his bag. One of his lovely sisters spotted the disposable camera and thought she would do him a good turn and take it to the chemist to be developed. When the photos were returned, his sister nearly fainted when she saw the content! Not sure where the photos are now.

Signed by Virgin

It's now January 1981 and we have played two gigs already. They had gone really well. We introduced everyone to 'Love Song', a song which went on to top charts all over the world, and it was evident that we had something right. We still needed to sort out our differences with Arista Records and sever the ties as soon as possible. Virgin Records were waiting in the wings, and we didn't want to lose their interest. Up till now we felt that Arista had failed to support us adequately. At one stage we put Bruce Findlay's head firmly on the chopping board, and wanted him out. Luckily Bruce could talk us out of anything, and he therefore remained our strong supporter and leader. But we refused to take Arista's indifference to us and we set our minds fully on targeting a deal with Virgin Records. By February we were gleefully putting pen to paper for a new contract.

We went into CaVa Studios in Glasgow, to demo song ideas. Richard Branson and his cousin, Simon Draper, came to Glasgow to meet up with us. They were great fun, especially Richard who gave us the impression that he was in league with the devil. Of course, he wasn't really, but we would find out in the future how much of a daredevil he could be! We shouted out a big thank you to Ross Stapleton, our new man at Virgin Records, who made this a reality.

We were unbelievably prolific at writing at this time, and showed it in our next album – or should I say albums. It was April 1981 when we arrived at the Farmyard Studios in Little Chalfont to start recording with our new producer Steve 'Old Cabbage Head' Hillage. What a genius of a man.

In May we release 'The American' on the Virgin label, which reaches the giddy heights of 59. That makes it a hit, as hits were determined up to Number 75 in the charts back then. Well done, Steve and the team at Virgin Records. Our recording was now going like wildfire. We keep throwing in new songs and, like a well-oiled machine unit, we reach the point of having too many songs! Steve can't decide what to leave out. We are now in the Townhouse Studios on Goldhawk Road, London. BBC Scotland want to do an interview with us working in the studio. B.A. Robertson, the Scottish musician and composer, often seen on *Top of the*

Steve Hillage admiring Derek's Peter Gabriel Europe tour T-shirt

Derek, Dicey O'Neil and Ian Reekie – old friends and bandmates

Jaine Henderson and Jim Kerr asleep on the Simple Minds tour bus – Mick MacNeil behind

Shirley McGee, friend and Jaine Henderson, lighting techie for Simple Minds

Derek 'vampire' Forbes with Peter Gabriel

Derek with Simple Minds supporting Peter Gabriel, 1980

Charlie Burchill, the van, and Big Dougie

Charlie 'piranha' Burchill and Jim 'Bob' Kerr

Jim Kerr, on tour with Simple Minds, Germany

Charlie Burchill and Mick MacNeil relaxing on the tour bus

Bruce 'I'm prepared to do what it takes' Findlay and Robert White, Simple Minds management, at the Marquee

Tour management team with Jaine Henderson, Eddie Cairns, Charlie Burchill and Brian McGee

Derek on tour with Simple Minds, Lyon, March 1983

Derek on tour with Simple Minds, Montpellier, 1983

Fans

John Leckie, Mick MacNeil and Charlie Burchill

Derek on tour with Simple Minds, a hotel room, New York, 1984

Ginger Baker's tour bus, sabotaged by Simple Minds

Ginger Baker's tour bus – Simple Minds wrote 'Younger, Prettier, Louder' on the side of the bus

Derek on tour with Simple Minds, Germany

Mick MacNeil, Charlie Burchill and Brian McGee on tour with Simple Minds, Germany

Jim Kerr, Derek and Charlie Burchill with fans

Simple Minds on tour with fans

Mel Gaynor and Derek, on tour with Simple Minds, Paris

Charlie Burchill, Richard 'Kid' Strange, Doctors of Madness, and Derek

Charlie Burchill, Brian McGee and Mick MacNeil find a Dutch Lottery Ticket

Ray Stock, our plugger, with Derek and Charlie Burchill backstage

Simple Minds – daring to dream

Derek, FourGoodMen

Simple Minds on tour, Bologna

Pops and known for his album *Shadow of a Thin Man*, is brimming with confidence as he enters the control room. Steve Hillage is hunched over the mixing desk, listening out for discrepancies in passages of music. B.A. bursts into the door with the camera team following behind. Steve doesn't even turn around, just shouts at the top of his voice, 'Out!' – and B.A. and all tiptoe straight back out. Did we laugh? You're fuckin' right we did!

We recorded 'Theme for Great Cities' at Park Gates Studio. We must have played it about 20 times before Steve decided on the optimum take. It has become an iconic part of Simple Minds history. Not long after this Jim went in to do vocals on another song, and Brian McGee came into the control room with Mick, Charlie and myself. Brian was wearing a dressing gown and slippers, and lay down on a big leather chair. Jim could see us all there in the room while singing take after take of whatever song it was. Jim saw Brian and by now, he was sleeping on the chair. Jim shouted: 'Get him the fuck out of here', and Brian woke up and left us to get on with the recording.

After we finished at Park Gates, we went to Regent's Park Studios in London for more vocals. I would go into the office and write funny poetry for the band, creating characters for their amusement. I felt that there was something obviously preying on Brian's mind.

Ken Lockie, the singer from Cowboys International, came to see us at the studio. Jim wanted Ken to help with some vocal parts. The song they were working on was '70 Cities (as love brings the fall)'. I had invited Kirsty MacColl up to see me and it was the first time we met. She brought me a lovely piece of the old sky smoke, which went down a treat. Now that she was there, Kirsty was invited to sing on '70 Cities (as love brings the fall)'. She sang beautifully, and her voice and Ken's brought the chorus to life. Kirsty and I had both been signed to Stiff Records in the late '70s, along with Madness.

Next day we sat around the control room listening to Steve's latest rough mixes. It was now time for a tea break. There was a weird atmosphere brewing in the studio, and the cause was about to be revealed. It was now that Brian announced he was leaving the band. It had all become too much: he missed his family, and his girlfriend, Shirley. They had been school sweethearts, and they were tighter than a Fifer's wallet. It was a sad, sad day, the end of a partnership, and it stung. We took a while to settle down as a new unit.

The next bit of bad luck followed at Townhouse Studios. Steve Hillage was beavering away, getting hardly any sleep, and took a bad turn – a suspected heart attack. Turned out that it wasn't as bad as first thought, but the stress had gotten to him, and he needed to calm down. Trooper that he was, he returned to the studio eager to carry on with the mixing. We had two albums of songs, and so we ended doing a double album, which would be split after the initial run had sold. Jim called them *Sons and Fascination* and *Sister Feelings Call*. They are the most innovative of all the albums we made, an incredible body of work.

By the time August came, we would have a new drummer and a new single, 'Love Song'. Kenny Hyslop took up the drum throne. In September *Sons and Fascination* was released along with *Sister Feelings Call*, which was deemed a bonus album. Not in our eyes. Both albums were part of the strong beating heart of Simple Minds.

We did a show at the Hammersmith Odeon, which was recorded by Virgin. Our tour has been planned, to start in Canada, then the United States and on into Australia.

Jim and I had a TV interview. We were young and I was nervous, while Jim just got on with it like a pro, albeit with a Scottish/mid Atlantic style accent, which he developed as the years passed.

Kenny Hyslop, our new drummer, turns out to be a genius behind the kit. Brian was exceptional, but Kenny uses a drum machine at the same time as playing the kit. We're going down a storm here. Though at one show – Le Shoeclack Dechaine, Quebec – Kenny had technical problems with his drums, which meant we couldn't do an encore. Some people complained that the show was too short but loved it anyway.

On 25 October, we play at the Concert Hall in Toronto. Peter Gabriel is playing at Maple Leaf Gardens, and he comes along to catch up with us. It's great to see him again. The next gig is a bit further to travel, so we don't play for three days. And it's getting colder by the day. Our gig was a crowd-pleaser again.

Early afternoon we were flying to Regina, and there seems to be a problem. Kenny and Bruce are nowhere to be seen. We board the plane and time is running out. A message comes through that Kenny has been arrested for leaving a store without paying for goods – a pair of socks and some aftershave. At the police station Bruce eventually manages to pay the police a $100 fine to have Kenny released. Meanwhile the rest of the band are on the plane trying to figure out a way for us to play the gig using a drum machine. A sheepish Kenny and Bruce finally board the plane. There was a sombre mood that night, very sombre! The next morning, we took a short flight to Saskatoon for the gig at Martinsville Hall. When we arrive, Mick, Charlie and I have lunch and the conversation turns to the event of the day before. We are still mourning the loss of Brian McGee, and we want him back in the band; Kenny's jacket is now on a very shaky peg.

On 4 November, we play at the Commodore Ballroom for the very first time; a fantastic venue. This was the last gig to end our Canadian tour.

On to America, and Los Angeles, to play at the Whisky a Go Go. This was an early gig starting in the afternoon which meant we could go sightseeing afterwards. Or so we thought. We played the gig, it wasn't that well attended, and the dressing room had no drinks, no food, absolutely nothing! Where was our star treatment? We had standards!

Then we heard an argument coming from the stage area. Why was our crew breaking down the equipment and beginning the load out? It turned out they had booked us for two shows that day, and we were meant to be onstage again that evening. Our soundman, Frank Gallagher, was almost at blows with the guys from the Whisky. The workers phoned the owner of the Whisky, Mario Maglieri, a total icon. The Godfather of the Los Angeles music scene, and much more besides. He was on his way. He arrived dressed in the finest light blue, perfectly tailored Italian silk suit, highly polished shoes that you could see your face in, a shock of white hair, and dark sunglasses. And turned out to be the most accommodating and friendly person. He asked us: 'Whaddya want?' I told him that we had just driven down from San Francisco and there were no drinks or sandwiches for us and the crew, as is normal in a dressing room before and after a show. He said, 'Leave it with me', and in the blink of an eye, the dressing room was laden with food and drink, enough to choke a horse. We went on to play a blinder of a set, and the audience had swelled considerably the second time around.

In the morning we set off to the airport to board a jumbo, travelling second class to Australia on a 36-hour journey. After some hours, we landed in Hawaii to refuel and were allowed to go out into the airport lounge to stretch our legs. That's the only bit of Hawaii we got to see, and it was dark.

In Sydney, we checked into the Travelodge Motel at Bondi Junction and in our rooms, there were huge baskets of fruits, some of which were totally foreign to us at that time. One looked like a hairy green testicle – the humble kiwifruit, I think. Our baskets were surrounded by other delicacies, like Vegemite and Malted Milk, and a host of sweets, no Maynards Sours though.

We went out to Bondi Beach – and all I saw was a schoolmate of mine, Frank Sallie, walking towards me. Frank had left Castlemilk years earlier and had been at my house to say farewell the night before he left. He said that he could spot a Pom a mile away by just looking out for the blue face.

Later I met up with another mate from school, Steve 'Stef' McIntyre; I'd stayed overnight at his house in Castlemilk the night before he left for Australia, a year or two before Frank. We drove around in his car; I was too hot, so I rolled the window down – and it was like a furnace outside. He told me to close it and turned on the air con until the car was freezing.

On the tour with Icehouse, we had an old rickety bus, with a toilet at the back. Everyone piled on – the full complement of Simple Minds, Icehouse and the Divinyls with Chrissy Amphlett on vocal duty, plus our crew. Bruce Findlay had brought along his 80-year-old Uncle Albert, just to get him out of the house. What a character! He would complain about absolutely everything, but he was so funny, and a real old gentleman at heart. Sometimes we would leave the old man at the hotel with Jane Findlay, Bruce's wife, so that we could go off into the bush on a quick gigging spree.

Working with Icehouse was great. They were huge in Australia, attracting lots of screaming and women fainting at the mere sight of Iva Davies. Our first gig in Australia was in New South Wales and I was overwhelmed by the reception.

In Brisbane, we played at the Cloudlands Ballroom, which looked like a big flying saucer, and you could see the venue's lights for miles. I bought an American Navy string vest from a great little antique shop which I wore onstage to keep me cool, I was as thin as a racing snake in those early days. I also wore my girlfriend's brown leather suit, which looked incredible but was too hot. The temperatures were almost unbearable. Bruce Findlay and I would hide in a bar all day so that we could be out of the sun, but we bought tablets that promised to tan our skin. Instead, we turned a lovely shade of orange, even the palms of our hands.

As we travelled through Australia on the big bus, we made a stop for one of our roadies whose father was buried along the route. The place was called Wagga Wagga, an Aboriginal name meaning 'place of many crows'. Our roadie lay on his father's flat gravestone.

We finished the tour with Icehouse, and then, due to public demand for our lovely selves, we decided to stay on and do some gigs by ourselves. We had a Toyota jeep for us to travel in, and a van with gear driving behind. We had great fun watching kangaroos jumping out of the bushes and hopping speedily in front of our vehicles, and we also saw camels! I never knew that camels were so prevalent in Australia, and that some of the locals used them for racing.

We played a small tour's worth of gigs starting in Canberra. I can't put my finger on why Canberra audiences loved us, but our reception was raucous.

On the road we met lots of Australian bands, including Hunters & Collectors and Midnight Oil. And INXS; we became pals with them.

The night before the last gig, Bruce Findlay called a meeting for us all in his room. Bruce started the meeting with record company stuff, and plans for the coming year. Kenny Hyslop was standing at the back of a couch fiddling with a ghetto blaster. Suddenly music exploded in the room. Kenny had pressed a button and all hell broke loose. Bruce shouted 'Kenny … dinny!' He tried to continue the meeting, but Kenny blasted out the sound again, Bruce was livid and screamed at Kenny, who said, 'I'm just trying to get down, Bruce.' The meeting ended with Kenny dancing to the music himself – but for Kenny the end was nigh.

After our final gig, 13 December, it was home for a few days, then back at the airport, for the next stop: Spain, and two shows at Rock-Ola in Madrid. Weather conditions at Gatwick meant our flight was delayed. Then we found out that Charlie's gear was trashed on the plane journey. He managed to give it a rub-down with a bit of Number 2 sandpaper and a half roll of gaffer tape to sort it out. Well done, wee Bangy. We made it onstage late, but the Spanish crowd still loved it.

Two days in Madrid was a great tonic for the band and we managed to get home in time for Christmas. On 26–28 December we played in Auld Reekie, aka Edinburgh, at the Nite Club. The last gig of the year was Tiffany's in Glasgow, and it was packed. You couldn't swing a cat if you tried.

'Glittering Prize' and *New Gold Dream*

In the New Year, we headed to Rockfield Studio in Wales to write songs for the next album. This was the last time any band used the Old Mill for rehearsals, as it was being turned back into a studio, to be named Monnow Valley. The songs were becoming more formed. I remember starting to play slap bass and my thumb was now in bits – though it didn't stop me.

The owner of Rockfield, Charles Ward, kindly bought us a video recorder, so the lads decided to hire out some videos and we watched *The Man Who Fell to Earth* with David Bowie. It's a great film, certainly better than the porno the lads hired next time. One night we all decided to go to the pub and bumped into none other than Robert Plant, who was with the legend that is Phil Collins. Paul Kerr, being a cheeky chappy, wound up Robert Plant saying, 'You've got too much Led Zeppelin in your heid.' Wild stuff.

The new songs we were writing sounded amazing; ideas were flowing and there were some great suggestions for singles. We were now rehearsing the new songs, and on 28 January my best mate Ian Reekie came down with my other long-time mate, Brian McLintock. They were coming to pick me up and drive me back for my duties as best man for Reekie at his wedding to Carolyn. The next day we headed to Glasgow, then Reekie dropped us off for a cab as he had to pick up an Alfa Romeo for his wedding getaway. Kay and I dropped Kenny off at his house in the West End. I had a bath in readiness for tomorrow's wedding, shitting myself about the speech. Sure enough, I'm delivering my best speech, reading out the cards and trying to tell jokes when one backfired. I am a huge Peter Cook and Dudley Moore fan, and tried the old Derek and Clive 'Blind' skit. Unfortunately, one of the guests was blind. Great wedding, though.

I ended up in the Warehouse Club in Glasgow where I met up with the happy couple and went to their house for dinner, then off to the disco at the Eglington Arms in Eaglesham. The next day I dropped the newlyweds at Edinburgh airport to see them off on honeymoon. My last task as best man was to deliver Reekie's new Alfa Romeo to his mother-in-law's house.

Early in February, Paul Kerr drove Charlie Burchill and myself to the bank in Edinburgh, where we opened new bank accounts – we were almost grown-ups! On 8 February I took the train from Glasgow to

London to meet up with the band, and when we went to our hotel we found out that our old mates from the Teardrop Explodes and Human League were staying there too. Of course we stayed up all night talking and getting pissed.

Rehearsals started on 9 February at Nomis Studios, where we ran through the set which was in good order. The next day, we headed to the EMI KPM Studios in Denmark Street to demo 'Promised You a Miracle'. We ran through the song, then put it down on tape. The result was fantastic – and our publishers from EMI, Phil and Alan, loved the track. There was a good buzz for this song.

We were currently Number 13 in Sweden with 'Sweat in Bullet', and the album was sitting at Number 17. On 11 February we did the David 'Kid' Jensen Show at BBC Maida Vale and recorded three tracks: 'In Trance As Mission', 'Promised You A Miracle' and 'King is White and in the Crowd'. Charlie, Mick, Paul and I stayed at the studio until half past three, and then left for a kebab. Friday 12 February we are off to Townhouse Studios by taxi to play 'Promised You A Miracle'. I'm fuckin' shattered. We put down the takes with Pete Walsh at the desk. The bass and drum sounds are excellent. Back at Columbia I met up with Positive Noise. Saturday, we went into the studio to work on 'Promised you a Miracle', where Mick put an incredible keyboard part onto the track. It is now sounding even better. We are working and perspiring so hard in the control room that it smells absolutely minging. While the rough mixing was going on, we watched television most of the time. On 14 February, Valentine's Day of course, it's the final mix of 'Promised You a Miracle'. I missed breakfast that morning and arrived at the studio at around half past two. The mix sounded fantastic, and we were on course to finish sometime in the small wee hours of the next morning. Our old friend, Iva Davies of Icehouse, came down with the record company good guys, Ray Hearn and Ross Stapleton. We stuffed our faces and watched our videos.

We were booked to go to the John Peel Session (which usually consisted of four songs) at BBC Maida Vale Studios on Delaware Road on 15 February. I got up at 1.45 p.m. (was never an early riser) after being up all night, then got a cab to BBC Maida Vale. Our four songs were 'Love Song', 'Promised You a Miracle', 'Sons and Fascination' and 'King is White and in the Crowd'. John Leckie was there, as was Ronnie Gurr, Ross Stapleton, Adam Sweeting from the *Melody Maker*, and Keith Bourton, then our press officer at Virgin.

Tuesday, 16 February we are still mixing the tracks at BBC Maida Vale, then back to the hotel for a sleep, and later we go out for food with Mick. In the evening, we go to a club to see Gina X, whom we knew from our travels in Germany, and the band Fashion. We get very pissed (surprise) and missed most of the show. We spoke to Ross Middleton from Positive Noise, and my good friend Ray McVeigh. Martin Kemp of 'Spandau Welder', our nickname for the band, is also there.

The next day, we're heading to Sweden for the European tour. We got up at 6 a.m., never an easy time to get up, and headed to Felixstowe for the ferry. It was a rough crossing and I remember hearing horses screaming from a trailer on the car deck. When we arrived, we took over an hour to clear customs (oh happy days) and they took our minibus apart.

On 19 February we arrived at the Karen Theatre, Gothenburg for a soundcheck. It's a really big venue with an excellent stage. This show was taped for Swedish radio. After the gig we went to Gallagher's Gay Bar, where we all made merry. On Saturday we headed to Stockholm, and a gig that saw us leaving the stage three times because a group of skinheads were punching people at the front when we started playing. There were bottles and saucers thrown onstage. I had a chair leg placed against my bass amp; just in case it got even more rowdy. Our promoter, 'Tuna', went on and spoke to the audience telling them to calm the fuck down. We managed to survive this gig, but that was more luck than control.

Next stops: Denmark, Germany, Holland. From Copenhagen we take the ferry across the Baltic Sea to Puttgarden, and then Hamburg, drivve through Germany and over the border to the Netherlands, ending up in Arnhem. All this travel malarkey was knackering.

We played at the Stokvishal, Arnhem on 26 February. I did manage to go out cycling to Velp with Mick before the gig; it was freezing, and I was still frozen at the soundcheck and couldn't play well. Though the gig reaction was great, we were half asleep. We had one of our occasional and rare post-mortems after the show, which took an hour out of our day.

From Arnhem to Amsterdam to Rotterdam. Got up early again. Everyone was knackered though, and we had a crap journey to the hotel. The show was a complete sell-out, and we were rewarded with two encores. Most of our shows were now selling out. We stayed at the gig/club for more drinks and legal puff.

On Monday it was back to Germany. Easy wee journey to Hamburg. The gig was mobbed, and it turned out to be excellent. We were taken for a meal after the show, courtesy of our publishing company. I may be wrong, but I think this was the night where we went to a cocktail bar, and I was getting hammered on Mai Tais and Suffering Bastards. Incredible. My diary entry is a single word: 'Pished'.

Tuesday, it's Hamburg to Hannover. This wasn't a long journey. The gig was great, but the hall wasn't quite full. Wednesday, Hannover to Berlin – on the Paris to Warsaw train, an amazing experience. In the meantime, Jim, off on his own, needed to be at a radio station in Berlin for an early, live interview.

From Berlin to Cologne. We got there late in the afternoon, and without Mick for the soundcheck because he had left his passport in his case before he got on the plane, and had to go back and get it. Mick and Robert White missed the flight and had to follow later.

From Cologne to Bochum. We found out later that Kraftwerk had come to the show to see us. Saturday 6 March, off to Wiesbaden. One thing that stuck out about this gig was the number of great band posters all over the walls: Talking Heads, Steve Hillage, Madness, Squeeze, Gillan, etc. It was a great gig although the mixer blew up during the second encore.

Once we were packed up, we prepared to do an overnighter to Munich. These fuckin' all-nighters killed me. Gallagher and I tried to sleep, but when we arrived in Munich we were shattered. We did manage to grab some sleep at the hotel and by the evening felt amazing. Great gig. We were taken out for a meal, where Jim and Kenny had an argument and Jim threw a glass of Coke all over Kenny. Kenny, as cool as he was, just said, 'Ah well, keeps the flies down'. The vibes were really bad and Kenny's time appeared to be running out. It's a pity, as is he is such an incredibly talented drummer, and we wouldn't have had 'Promised You a Miracle' without him. Kenny was the inspiration.

Monday, and no one is talking to Kenny. Tuesday, we arrive in Lyon. I had a shower, wrote in my diary, and went out for a walk with Paul Kerr, Johnny Ramsay and Steve Pollard, looking for something to eat. In the evening I went out drinking with Charlie, Mick, Paul and Pete and later we meet up with a drunken Jim and Gallagher Kenny was nowhere to be seen.

Wednesday 10 March, and we've got a gig at the Palais d'Hiver. 'Love Song' is on the radio and find out we have gone gold in Sweden; we've sold 21,000 there since the tour.

We travelled to Clermont. The gig was empty. Lenny told us there was a side door at the back! We all burst out laughing: how the fuck could there be a side door at the back? We never let him forget that one.

Friday 12 March, we head to Paris, for a gig at the Place de Gabrielle, just off the Champs-Élysées. What a brilliant venue. Human League (they must have liked us) came to see us that night. After an incredible Parisian response, I ventured out after the show and had photos taken with a group of youngsters from Alabama. The next gig was in Rennes at the Espace, where we have one of our worst-ever responses. We don't know why and to top it all, I got food poisoning.

On Sunday 14 March, we did a TV show with Vincent Lamey. We were filmed for four hours solid at a beautiful old studio. We did six songs, six times each, and for every time we had a break, we had a Peruvian pick-me-up, every one of us. This footage is incredible and is probably up there with the best Simple Minds footage.

It's Monday, 15 March, the start of a new week, and we drive from Paris to Brussels and find out that Johnny Ramsay and Steve Pollard have crashed the truck on their way into Brussels. We immediately cancel that day's TV appearance. It turned out that both of them are alright, although very shaken. The gig that night is triumphant, and we're on a high knowing that our crew were OK.

After the last gig in Belgium we're glad to take the ferry to Dover and travel onwards to the Columbia Hotel in London for the night. At the hotel that night were the Stray Cats, ABC and DAF (Deutsche Amerikanische Freundschaft). The Columbia is a proper Rock & Roll hotel with many a story to be told – although I don't have one for you this time.

On Friday I got the train from Euston Station with Mick, Charlie and Paul and we were on our way home to Glasgow. By this time, Kenny's time with Simple Minds had just ended, to be replaced by Mike Ogletree.

We're now between tours, working on song rehearsals with Mike Ogletree, radio sessions and the occasional TV appearance.

On 29 March we were off again, back on the ferry to the Netherlands. We were booked to play, again, at the Paradiso in Amsterdam, and we stayed at the American Hotel, a beautiful old hotel popular with the jet set. As usual we set off on a hash hunt. The gig at the Paradiso was packed. We had played there many times before. Our friends from the Netherlands were there and we partied through the night. We were getting the band match fit for some bigger gigs now. We felt that we were now ready for festivals. On 11 April we played the Teatro Tenda in Bologna, Italy. The crowd was huge and we had an incredible reception. What a reception, what a venue! Italy had taken us to their heart.

Before heading to Germany for a festival, we had more rehearsals and writing. It was time for the next album and *New Gold Dream (81–82–83–84)*. Bruce Findlay had heard from a good friend in Edinburgh of a farm with a big barn and accommodation, where we could stay and record our demos. It was situated just outside Newburgh in Fife, and was owned by a slightly eccentric man called Will, who was always smiling, happy and helpful. There we wrote the music for 'Someone Somewhere (In Summertime)'. I am sure Jim also wrote more than a few ideas at this time. He would be sitting on top of my amplifier, an Ampeg SVT Classic amp and 8×10 Ampeg speaker cabinet, while we played and honed the songs into some semblance of order. Everything was set up for the session to start.

Paul Kerr was filming the sessions from day one with a gigantic camera the size of an Eastern European dodgy copy of a Walkman. Mike Ogletree was with us now and his cymbal work was astounding. He added to the good vibe of the songs on *New Gold Dream (81–82–83–84)*.

Once at dinnertime the chef – yes, we had a chef – asked us if we liked mushrooms. We all answered in the affirmative. So, dinner was beef bourguignon with mushrooms, and with a tottie on the side. We were all a bit jolly afterwards and had a few cigars and brandy. The chef asked if we liked mushroom tea. I had no idea but went ahead and tried a cup. My jolliness tripled in size. From then on we would have pizza with mushrooms, steak with mushrooms, mushroom soup and any other variation the chef could think of, as long as it included mushrooms! I had quite a heated discussion with Jim under the mushroom influence, and I couldn't stop laughing while Jim was very serious indeed. To his credit he knew that it was the mushrooms that had taken over.

The songs were sounding incredible now; our excitement was building, and we really felt we had something very special. We decided to make a couple of videos to capture it all. I was dressed up like Midge Ure and Jim was standing behind one of Mick's keyboards looking every inch the doppelgänger of Ultravox's Billy Currie, so we made a video of 'Vienna', which was hilarious. I also did a David Sylvian impersonation of 'Ghosts' video too.

At some point the sessions were interrupted – and what a welcome interruption it was.

* * *

Before I tell you about it, let me take you back to a gig at West Runton Pavillion in England. There was not a massive crowd, and after the show, we were a bit downhearted. Then Bruce Findlay came bouncing in, in his normal jaunty manner, and proceeded to pick us all up. We started exchanging ideas about maybe writing a single and releasing it before we had written an album. We all felt that we needed to boost our popularity, and if we had something to excite the record company and bring them onboard with the idea, we could make a definite push to expand our audience.

Kenny Hyslop had recorded a lot of Black radio stations when we had been on tour in the States, particularly New York, and he had a snippet of music that we all instantly liked. It was the first four notes that set me off on my funky bass line route, and so with the help of Mick, Charlie and Kenny on drums, we came up with the music, and Jim followed with lyrics later. We had the song we needed for our 'single' plan to work.

Back to the interruption: we had just received a phone call from Virgin Records telling us that we were to play *Top of the Pops*! We had to drop everything and leave for London straightaway. I, of course, had to look out my best hairstyle and buy some clothes for the show. Our drummer, Mike Ogletree, had never played the track with us; it was Kenny Hyslop who was on the recording. We get to the studio. It was our turn to go on and the TV engineers left the microphones on for a bit of audience sound to add to the ambience. This meant you could hear the drums along with the playback of the song, as we were miming, which was normal for *Top of the Pops*. We could hear Mike's drums marginally out of time with the playback, but we survived. We left quite sharply after the show to watch Mel Gaynor play with Imagination in Slough. Mel was recommended to us by Peter Walsh, our chosen producer for *New Gold Dream (81–82–83–84)*.

It was now June 1982 and we were ready for our first open air festival at the Schüttorf Festival, Münster. Bruce Findlay brought his friend

Kevin Coyne, an alternative rock singer, songwriter, poet and filmmaker. He was some man and very entertaining.

There were caravans parked in the backstage area and we piled in to get ourselves ready. The headline act was Frank Zappa. He did a press interview outside in the backstage area. He had a giant of a man as security beside him, as he sat on a chair in the centre of a circle of journalists. The journos fired questions at him and the Zappster fired answers back.

Time for our gig. We looked out at a sea of people, probably most of which hadn't heard us yet. The gods were with us that night and we went down well.

Back at Rockfield Studios for the start of recording for *New Gold Dream (81–82–83–84)*. After we had recorded most of the tracks, it was time to put down Jim's vocals. We had never heard any of the lyrics or melodies, so everything that was being recorded was new to us. It was a beautiful sunny day in Oxfordshire, and the sun was glinting on the lake that Richard Branson had put in for clients, stocking it with loads of Canadian trout for a bit of fishing, should anyone feel like it. On top of that, Richard had added a pair of stunning Whooper swans.

On the morning of this wonderful day, Jim Kerr, lost in a dream, could be found sitting on the slope of the field, under the shade of an old oak tree, notebook and pencil in hand, jotting down and reworking lines for the songs of *New Gold Dream (81–82–83–84)*. It was a very peaceful sight, akin to a John Constable painting. The mood soon changed as one of the swans took umbrage at the trespassing Kerr and charged at him honking and hissing from its beak … Jim instinctively jumped up and ran, but the angry swan screeched up the recently mown lawn, chasing and taunting him relentlessly … 'It'll break your arm, Jim!' we shouted from the cheap seats like kids at a Saturday morning matinee at the local cinema. Jim ran towards the manor and eventually the swan gave up and assumed victory.

Pete Walsh put down his Pimm's and announced that he required Jim for vocal duties, so they both made their way into the studio to make a start. Vocals were usually recorded with only the producer and singer. This rule goes back to when Brian McGee turned up in the studio during the recording of *Sons and Fascination* wearing a dressing gown and a pair of slippers, and Jim remarked most definitely 'get him the fuck out of here'. I digress. This would be a long process and we weren't needed until the songs were properly structured.

As the recording was going on, we could hear everything from our rooms at the manor. We conversed through opened windows. Mick MacNeil, our sound engineer, Frank Gallagher and I were debating the songs and critiquing their progress. Gallagher: 'Turn that fuckin' noise down, for fuck sake.' MacNeil: 'Aw naw ... he's fuckin' ruining ma music.' Me: 'No' too bad ... ye canny whistle that up a ladder, though!' Things turned out alright in the end.

On a break from the recording, we decided to have a good old-fashioned blowout. During that day Mike Ogletree had invited his girlfriend, Eddi Reader, to the studio. Eddi is a very talented Scottish singer-songwriter. 'The night drave on wi' sangs and clatter; / And ay the ale was growing better'! There we were, smoking personality cigarettes and downing mandies and making a serious dent on good old Richard Branson's wine collection, the final count being 20 bottles of red and 21 bottles of white. What a fun time!

I was dressed in an all-white Katharine Hamnett ensemble. I was so pissed and feeling like rubber due to the intake of the old mandies that I decided to walk down near the lake. I walked right down the slope and suddenly I was up to my chest in water. There was a lot of algae, and I was now covered in it. Fuck me, did that cold water wake me up! Luckily, I didn't harm myself, but my clothes were now green ... Undeterred, I changed and carried on until the wee hours of the morning.

We all enjoyed being at the manor. When dinner was served, we would eat as much as we liked and we would often have a food fight. Richard, of course, joined in. All it took was for one of us to fire a hot potato at someone and all hell broke loose. After dinner we would retire to the lounge.

As a bass player, I would often have quite a bit of spare time on my hands, having finished second after the drum tracks were finished. I only had to do some overdubs towards the end of recording and just before the mixing process. I would go into the recording room when the mix was being done and I would play on the piano, or drums, or Hungarian nose flute, if Jim wasn't using it, but he was still hanging on in there with the trombone lessons, like a man possessed. I would go into the office and use the typewriter, and I would write poems, silly nonsense poems, and illustrate them with my cartoon character, Dan-yer-man.

Derek in the studio working on his tunes

Steadying the Ship

By July, it was pretty evident that Mike wasn't cutting it for us in the drum department. Mike is an amazing drummer, but it seemed to be all going much too fast for him. Mel Gaynor was called in to steady the ship. He arrived like a thunderstorm. In the past it had been a sheer joy playing in the same room as both Mel and Mike, facing each other on two drum kits, with me in the middle on bass, recording the backing track for the song 'New Gold Dream'. It was euphoric. My ears are still ringing. There was the drum machine playing too, with all three of us keeping bang on time to the beat. The Simple Minds tank division was now in the building.

We were booked into Air Studios on Oxford Circus to work on 'Glittering Prize' as the new single. It was only Charlie Burchill and I there representing the rest of the band. Charlie still had his arm in plaster at this point, from his fingers to his elbow. Apparently, Charlie and his girlfriend Carol had a juggling cat. It was juggling a carving knife and when Charlie went to take the blade away, he caught the sharp end, which sliced through one of his fingers! Charlie got himself to hospital and had it stitched back together. That's the story I've heard. For a while we thought the tour could be in jeopardy, but Charlie soldiered on.

As we entered the studio, we saw Jeff Lynn from the Electric Light Orchestra in the corridor. Brian McGee would have pissed himself with excitement if he had been there. Charlie and I were in the control room listening to the playback when Linda McCartney walked in and asked if we would like to meet Paul. Now it was my turn to, almost, wet myself. We followed Linda into the control room, where Paul was working on the album *Tug of War*. He was putting down a vocal. He danced about as he sang, and he wasn't wearing shoes, just socks. At the desk was George Martin, and beside him was Mike 'McGear' McCartney, Paul's younger brother. Linda's daughter, Heather, was there too and was very excited to see us, which was strange. We went into the green room with Linda and Paul, and Paul could see me shaking and he asked me why. I told him about my sister Elizabeth having all the early Beatles records, which blasted out of her room day and night, and that my mother was a nurse at one of their gigs in Glasgow and how this had influenced by interest in music. I had a Beatles pass which a journalist had given me earlier and it was signed by Tony Barrow, their press officer. Paul noticed it and signed my pass: 'Paul McCartney to a very Simple Mind'; he signed Charlie's plaster cast: 'Paul McCartney in the groove'.

New Gold Dream Tour

New Gold Dream was released in September to incredible and generous praise. Our *New Gold Dream* tour was just around the corner and as part of the campaign HMV, Oxford Street was sporting huge window-sized posters of individual photos of us in its windows. It was incredible to see.

Our record company, Virgin, purchased our back catalogue from Arista and reissued a version of *Real to Real Cacophony* in October.

We started the *New Gold Dream* tour on 3 September 1982 with a single show in Helsinki, Finland! Not only did the place have a bit of a Cold War feel to it but, to cap it all, the hotel minibar was totally empty, not even a Britvic Orange. The gig was partially recorded and broadcast by the Finnish Broadcast Company (YLE). The tracks were mostly from *New Gold Dream* except for 'The American'.

Then it was back to Edinburgh, Sheffield, London – management keeping us working on a tight schedule. Next stop Reading and then we had a day off and flew to Belgium for a TV show (as you do). Our crew had the night off in Brighton. They parked their trucks and buses along the seafront. They needed some time out; there had been quite a lot of friction in the camp. But there was trouble in Brighton! The crew were back on the bus, in their bunks, when some strange guy came onboard and threw a punch at our lighting fairy Steve Pollard, and more guys followed him onto the bus. Big Johnny Ramsay grabbed two of them and took them outside and sat on them, while throwing a punch or two. The crew set about the rest of the intruders. Pete 'Basic' was a hero that night. Matt Dunn, Paul Kerr and the others also sorted these bawbags out and harmony reigned again. We were oblivious to all this, miming at a TV show in Belgium with Orchestral Manoeuvres in the Dark.

The next day we flew back for the gig, spotted the odd black eye and bruise among the crew, and heard the story of The Battle of Brighton.

We played the gig, which went down a storm, and then all trundled back to the Grand Hotel. In the morning we had breakfast with Joe Brown, the '60s pop star and thoroughly nice guy. Then we moved on to Friars in Aylesbury, where ducks are nervous. This was our last gig on the UK part of the tour.

Time for another jaunt to Oz, followed by New Zealand and two gigs in Auckland. Wow, what a place Auckland is, it had a real vibe going on, a bit of a hard edge, but extremely beautiful if you looked around

Stevie Pollard, Derek and Wendy

the edges. The gigs were punkier than we imagined and the audiences a bit more hip. Both gigs went well, and we felt we were a success there. On the 20th and 21st we were in Wellington and then Palmerston, but I have no idea which venues we played while there. We just kept going on this marathon. Our next stop is Canada.

The lifestyle was now becoming rather manic, but at the time I wouldn't have had it any other way. The Commodore Ballroom is always a fantastic venue.

We are being supported for this part of the tour by Visible Targets, a new wave band from Seattle, Washington. We played Edmonton, Calgary, and the Student Union in Saskatchewan – a bit of a nightmare. The gig doubled up as a Halloween gig and the students came in fancy dress. There were lasses with fishbowls on their heads shooting us with ray guns and the like; just not a rock gig at all. Unfortunately, a couple of the audience were dressed as the Ku Klux Klan, which left us all raging. We didn't want to play until the fuckers had been ejected. We had a big fight with the promoter, Frank Weipert, in our dressing room. He was dressed as Dracula. We called him an asshole and he replied, 'Well, I may be an asshole, but I'm the biggest asshole in Canada!' So we tore him a new one. Later, he took Charlie and Mike out to explore some of the local nightlife, but they ended up being stopped by the police and Dracula was taken away, leaving Charlie and Mick by the side of the road. Mike later said that the tour was 'a fucking disaster, but riveting. Dodgy equipment, dodgy trucks, a bus that was 20 years out of date. It was a *Heart of Darkness* feeling.'

Next day Dracula left a secret package of enjoyment dust for each of us, thank you.

The next gigs took us to Winnipeg (freezing), Guelph, Ottawa, and Montreal. On 6 November, we arrive in Toronto for two gigs, the second being Mike Ogletree's last gig with the band. We were changing drummers again and Mel Gaynor would be in the drumming seat when we returned to the UK. The powers that be felt Mike's drumming style didn't quite fit with the band. The last gigs in Toronto, Canada were amazing, and then we flew back to Glasgow.

After a wee break and a bit of R & R, we start off with two nights at Tiffany's in Glasgow on the 18 and 19 of November. The 18th is a red-letter day for the band and Simple Minds fans: it was Mel's first gig, and we rocked! We now had our little brothers, China Crisis, on board for the tour. They are extremely funny, but then Scousers are very funny. Tiffany's was a hoot. I met a young Gavin Mitchell, aka Boaby the Barman, from the Scottish TV series *Still Game*, outside the venue at soundcheck time. His brother called me over as I was going inside, and he told me that his younger brother had left his ticket in his jeans and washed them and no longer had a ticket to show. I said, Worry ye not, I will stick him on the guest list, and in fact, I'll take him into the soundcheck with me, which I did. I put my bass on him and let him bang out a tune. Then I took him into the dressing room and introduced him to the band. He hasn't forgotten that day. The two gigs were raucous.

The next day we were back again at one of my favourite venues, Newcastle City Hall, for a gig, which was filmed for Italian TV and shown on BBC too. You can still watch this online. We cross the water for a gig on 22 November at Ulster Hall, in Belfast. We went down a storm there that night! The next day, it was the turn of St Francis Xavier Hall, in Dublin – an incredible night in the city, always a pleasure.

Back to England, and Leeds, Manchester and Liverpool, the Royal Court. Always a top venue, and a top audience. Though our PA broke down, we soldiered on and completed the set and I'm not sure anyone noticed.

On St Andrew's Day, 30 November, we play at the Top Rank in Cardiff to a great Welsh welcome. Exeter University, on 1 December, was one of the best gigs on the tour. Oxford next – the Apollo, just up the road from the Manor Studios where we recorded the album. Then Brighton Dome, a great place to play. A day off, and we go to the Gaumont in Ipswich. Ipswich Town football team came up to the dressing room to see us after the show. I met a young Terry Butcher, whom I was lucky enough to play a couple of games of football with later on, and also John Wark, the Liverpool and Scotland legend, whom I befriended after the show.

Back to London, and the Lyceum, Strand. Just incredible, lots of pals and well kenned faces. Then a particularly spectacular gig at King's Hall, Stoke-on-Trent on 9 December; amazing, that's all I can say. The Odeon in Birmingham on 10 December – a great audience as usual, and our old friend, the guitar player from Duran Duran, appeared again; he must have liked us a lot.

Gigs followed in Birmingham, Leicester, Bristol, Sheffield and Derby before we headed back north to Scotland. When I was doing so many gigs, one after the other, I always thought of the Beatles traipsing across the country, and it inspired me to keep going.

Back up north now to Dundee (still with China Crisis) for a gig at Caird Hall. Mick did a great recording of this one. Then a gig at the Capital Theatre in Aberdeen, and back to Edinburgh for a gig at the Playhouse. The Christmas crowds were out for this one. As you know, Simple Minds cut their teeth here in the beginning, and Auld Reekie will never let us down. Returning to Glasgow we did two shows at Tiffany's to end this part of the *New Gold Dream* tour.

The year had been one of absolute madness, fun and outrageous days. We were exhausted. A big thank you to everyone who helped the band make it through this incredible year! You know who you are, and I love you all.

Time Out and Then Back Again

It's 1 January and the band are dog-tired, asleep on our feet and ready to drop. Bruce had wanted to send us out again on a massive tour to the US and Canada straightaway, but Jim, Charlie and the rest of us needed a break. As an alternative, Bruce booked us into a studio in South Thoresby, Lincolnshire for a couple of months of writing and recording. So, we took a well-earned break from travelling for a couple of months and started to work on new material.

The nearest big town was Louth, and Grimsby, the Las Vegas of Lincolnshire, was the next most accessible fun town, should we want a night out. The studio was called The Chapel, and it was! A funny old place. Mr and Mrs Bram looked after us, and they were lovely old souls. Mrs Bram would call us with the cry, 'there's yer dinner, ducks.'

There was a pub next to the studio where we would go in the evenings. There, we discovered some new drink, and we young ducks took a fancy to them. Guinness and Dubonnet, or Guinness & Black (blackcurrant). The business! It was also around this time that we changed our gig rider to include Bourbon, Jack Daniel's or Jim Beam.

There were some special tracks being created at the Chapel. Charlie was producing some great sounds: he had more pedals than the whole cast of the Tour de France, and he was going to use them. Mick was on fire too, and we could be relied on to produce the goods. Jim preferred to write lyrics on his own and would disappear to his room to assemble them in a coherent order in his notebook before revealing the result to the rest of us. Bruce had often, over the years, sent Jim away on his own for inspiration.

March was approaching and the next part of the *New Gold Dream* tour was imminent.

The first and last European gigs for *New Gold Dream* tour were all in March. We gigged in the Netherlands, Belgium, the Netherlands (again), France, Italy, Germany, Denmark, Sweden, Norway, and Sweden again for the last gig on 29 March. It was hectic.

Our first gig of that month was at the Royal Theatre Carré in Amsterdam. Sister Sledge had played the night before. It was one of the smarter-looking venues on the circuit but may have been wrong for us. The gig was great, but we got that London Palladium vibe. The next day we were at the Cirque Royal in Brussels for the first of two nights. Jim did an interview in his room, speaking in his whacky, mid-Atlantic, quasi-Glaswegian voice that he had perfected, and let the people know that he was keen to be driven around the wilderness in a big golden bus with a full tank of fuel. We had a laugh in the lift of the Metropole Hotel over that. It wasn't a mystery why Jim spoke like this: this was how he managed to lose his childhood stammer, which had plagued him in his youth and late teens. He had a wild sense of humour and would joke about it, even self-naming himself Fred McMutter.

We all had names for each other. Mick was known as Morag, Charlie was Charlie Pirahna, Brian was Leany or Greety McGee, Mel was the Cakeman, and I, last but not least, was Big Dan and sometimes Yacht Face, due to the large pyramidical feature on the front of my face. Now you see, as a band, we could be brutal with each other; it just depended who was on the end of the lashing tongues of our acid wit!

We had, and still have, an incredible number of Simple Minds fans in Belgium. It was always a favourite destination. The Metropole Hotel was where we would sit, of an afternoon, the sun shining and ordering Croque-monsieur and Croque Hawaii, along with some of the thousands of beers produced here.

Our next gigs took us through France: Paris, Rennes, Bordeaux. The journey out of Paris and into the wine regions is spectacular. Our tour bus glides through all of the leafy suburbs, and I sit on the bus at the window, reading signs and working out their origin. I always do this when travelling, linking Saxon, Viking, French and Latin, to names of towns and villages. On the 11 March, we are on our way south to Montpellier to a great little theatre. Then the Winter Palace, Palais d'Hiver in Lyon, our last gig in France for this tour.

We had a travel day coming up on the 13th: we were going to Italy to rekindle our love affair with the country. Little did we know the effect that the next gig at Palasport in Bologna would have. We had been the whipping boys of the Peter Gabriel Tour in our Italian gigs, but now things had changed. Our hard work was, at last, paying off. The gig stage was almost circular. I remember being able to walk around the stage and acknowledge the audience all around. The Italians, not only in Bologna, were the most hot-blooded audiences we had so far encountered – and they went wild that night. The show was recorded for posterity.

One hilarious moment happened to me onstage that night. We were using wireless systems for our guitars with specific frequencies. My Nady system suddenly had a change of heart and connected to a local taxi company. I heard the controller talking to customers and other drivers as I danced around, supposedly playing my bass guitar. It didn't last long, thank goodness. The audience would have heard everything loud and clear.

On 15 March we arrive in Rome. We have a day off and get a chance to see Rome. Of course, my bandmates, being quite cultured and religious, wanted to see the Vatican. There were lots of people waiting to get inside. I saw a woman who was being refused entry because her arms were uncovered. She was distraught, so I gave her my Simple Minds sweatshirt, and she managed to get in.

We ate in an incredible restaurant and sat outside for coffee and alcoholic beverages. I had absorbed the Italian atmosphere and I started speaking old Roman to my comrades. Mel joined in along with Mick and Charlie. It went something like this. I turned to Mel and said, 'Melus … checkus burdus … prettius.' He replied, 'Yesus Danus.' I said, 'Thinkus tartus?' His reply, 'Not us tartus, hookerus,' I reply in amazement, 'Hookerus? reallus?' Mel said, 'Yesus … penuslikus!' Our names that night were Danus, Melus, Charlus, Mickus and Jiminus Boylus. Almost as funny, but not quite, as Biggus Dickus and Incontinentia Buttocks …

After our Roman escapades it was time to head to the beautiful city of Milan. We have a meeting with the rep from Giorgio Armani: we are having a photoshoot with (can you believe it, us boys from Glasgow)

Italian *Vogue*, and are being endorsed by Armani. We now have stage clothes coming out of our ears. How lucky we were! We were built like racing snakes, then, so all the clothes fitted us well.

We then head to Deutschland and Munich. Another gig for us at the Deutsches Museum, a veritable home from home now. On the 21 March we go to Düsseldorf, to play at Phillipshalle, again as the main act. I remember having our auras cleansed by a self-proclaimed white witch in the dressing room before our performance. This daughter of Lilith would accompany us for a few weeks on that tour. I must say the cleansing really worked!

Our next gig was the Stadthalle Offenbach, the same venue where Peter Gabriel asked me to play bass, as John Giblin was stuck in traffic.

The next day we crossed the border, once again through Niemansland for the transit route between West Germany and Soviet-occupied East Germany. We made our way north to Puttgarden for the ferry to Denmark. We played in Copenhagen, a couple of nights in Stockholm and then a gig in Oslo at the Chateau Neuf. A wonderful place, though stupidly expensive. The gig was well attended and enthusiastically received. A beautiful woman with long black hair wanted to be my bass roadie, for real: she knew everything about the bass and the gear I was using. I obviously had my bass roadie, Andy Battye, who certainly wasn't pretty, but he was an incredible tech, and funny, so I had to politely decline. The last gig was in Sweden again, this time in Gothenburg. This was the last show of the Scandinavian run of gigs for *New Gold Dream*, and it was a rousing success.

It was the end of March, and we were already preparing to head to the United States in April. I wish I had been on an Air Mile rewards scheme!

The first week in April we visited the US Embassy in Grosvenor Square, London, to be interviewed for our work visas for the next part of the *New Gold Dream* tour. We flew, very lucky lads, first class to Los Angeles and were given some time off when we arrived to acclimatize ourselves to the eight-hour time difference before starting our run of shows.

I shared a room with Mick. For some reason we were the party room. One day we were entertaining some of the locals, two beautiful women, when there was a knock on the door. It was 'Mitch' Mitchell, the legendary drummer of Jimi Hendrix, accompanied by a tall blond woman who turned out to be a dealer of the old Peruvian marching kind. I nearly fell over. I opened the door and went down on my knees in a 'we are not worthy' pose. I was starstruck, but Mitch was such a nice guy that we were soon at ease and he told us stories about his time with Jimi.

In the days to come we walked about a lot in Hollywood, like a wandering gang, but in reality we were just a bunch of daft boys having a laugh, and heading to the nearest boozer. Charlie, Mick and I ended up at a tiny bar on the Strip. We asked for the best bourbon he had, and he produced an old bottle of Wild Turkey which was pure firewater with an unbelievable taste. We tested a few glasses of various types of bourbon, then made our way to the hotel. Los Angeles closes early, unless you have been invited to a party, so we mostly stayed in at the Sunset Marquis and jumped into the pool now and then. Grand Master Flash was staying there with his band, as were Tears for Fears and the Police. It was just a big music fest for us and the hotel residents. In the morning we would walk up the road to Ben Franks, the legendary diner in Hollywood, for fresh orange juice, hot coffee and French toast with bacon and maple syrup.

I also loved going into the Roosevelt Hotel, where Marilyn Monroe and Montgomery Clift reputedly haunt the corridors of the top floor. Some people say they hear the trumpet being played in the middle of the night by the ghostly Mr Clift. The cocktails are good, especially my favourite, the Old Fashioned. We would also wander along the Strip, past Grauman's Chinese Theatre, and look at the autographed hand and footprints in the sidewalk.

Mel hired a car, and we decided to go for a cruise along Sunset Boulevard. We get stopped by the LAPD, who tell Mel to get out of the car. We try to open the door but are told to stay inside. When satisfied that we are not a roaming gang, stealing a car, they let us go.

R & R at an end, we were now bound for Seattle, Washington, to play at the Eagles Hippodrome. Our support act was the Visible Targets again. They were a great band and would support us a lot when in the US.

The gig was packed, and we were still producing the goods. This was the gig where I was properly introduced to Mick Ronson; the first time we'd met was at Green's Playhouse, Glasgow, where we waved to each other. The show that night went really well, and the Visible Targets were really good too. They were locals, and their fans got right behind them. Mick was producing their album. At the hotel we got changed after the gig and went for a drink with the band and took over the rooftop bar. I was really surprised to see Mick Ronson at the bar, and I made a beeline for him. What a gem of a man Ronno was. We had a few drinks before being approached by one of our American roadies. He was a Vietnam vet, and I told him that a cousin of mine fought for the ANZACs in Vietnam. The guy passed me a little bottle of nasal spray, which, surprise surprise, contained a familiar liquid, which I tried and passed on to Ronno. He took a nose full (and between the two of us we could certainly pass as a couple of old Roman chaps), then asked, 'What do you think, Derek?' I replied that I wasn't sure and took another sniff: 'Maybe you could test it again, Ronno.'

That night Bruce Findlay and our lawyer/manager Robert White were sitting at a table having just had a late dinner. They offered me some red wine, and this time I was ready. It went down a treat.

We had been looking for co-management in the United States for the band. Cue the legendary Bill Graham – famed for the Fillmore, promoting the Rolling Stones, a cameo in *Apocalypse Now*, and much, much, more. We went to Bill's house, a stunning mansion just outside the city, as his guests – and by the end of our visit he was part of the Simple Minds team. We left San Francisco and headed back down to Hollywood. We played the Beverley Theatre on 15 April, one of the most prestigious venues in La La Land. At the end of the show, we walked out into the crowd and wandered around talking to various people we met. At one point I was with Jim, and we met up with Slim Jim Phantom and his new wife, Britt Ekland. I then met up with Sacha Newley and he joined us at a fantastic Beverly Hills restaurant that evening.

The gig was well attended and after the show we retired to the dressing room. I went outside the dressing room for a joint with Matt Dunn, drum roadie extraordinaire. The fire escape door opened, and in came a young man in a purple suit. Matt looked at him and said, 'Haw wee man, ye canny come in here the noo … the band are getting changed!' The young man turned and went back out the way he came. 'Who was that?' I asked Matt, but he didn't know either. It turned out it was Prince – and we had shown him the door.

17 April and we are picked up from the hotel by the limo. I am in the car with our manager Bruce, and Jim, Charlie, Mick and Mel. We are heading south to San Diego. One of us tapped the window between us and the driver and after a bit of coded parlance later we were passed a couple of small packages of the devil's dandruff. If we had asked for a lawnmower, a bespoke shave, or a bag of coconuts, I'm sure we would

have got that too. The only other place I know where you can hail a cab and get anything you want, was in Puerto Vallarta in Mexico.

The next gig was at the Fox Theatre. It's a lot bigger than the Belly Up Tavern in Solano Beach, where Mick MacNeil and I would play years later with our band FourGoodMen (the other two good men were Ian Donaldson and Bruce Watson). San Diego is a real music-loving town, with great audiences. American audiences in general are superb, whooping and a hollering all through the shows. We drive back up to Los Angeles and party into the night. We then have a few days to get to Houston Texas. The bus pulled up at the Sunset Marquis in the morning. Mick dished out the Irish coffees, and off we went.

We arrive in Houston, Texas on 22 April looking for South Fork, but we're in the wrong town for that. The gig tonight is at the Tower Theatre, which turns out to be a proper-looking theatre, perfect for a rock gig. Afterwards we were invited to a party that some lovely cowgirls had put on for us. I was taken into the bathroom by a big leggy brunette, who proceeded to use the toilet while chopping out a couple of lines for us. She was very matter-of-fact about the whole thing, and got up, buttoned her jeans and we went straight back into the party.

After our Texan adventure we headed for New Orleans. We were staying in the French Quarter on Bourbon Street, which was a bit mad. Each drink we had, we were given the glass with the bar's name on to keep as a souvenir. Not many survived the journey back to Glasgow, but it was a nice memento. We spotted cool old men tap dancing on the boardwalks as we made our way past great music clubs and bars. Jazz was certainly in the air here, and blues too. It was a wonderful place, unless of course, you strayed off the old beaten path. We were conned by a young man selling what we thought were rocks of the old Peruvian, but it turned out to be baking powder or some other shit. The guy was gone, and so was our money. All I could think of was Peter Fonda, Dennis Hopper, Karen Black and Toni Basil having a bad trip on acid in the graveyards around New Orleans, in *Easy Rider*.

We were now bound for Washington to play at the Ontario Theatre. Our support for the gig was Martha and the Muffins from Toronto, Canada. Their single 'Echo Beach' became a classic, and rightly so. We started our set with 'King is White and in the Crowd', for a change.

Next we were off to Cleveland Ohio at the Agora Ballroom. Who the actual fuck booked this tour? It was like throwing a dart at a map and playing wherever it landed. We had REM as support that night. Here we played at one of a chain of clubs dotted all over America, this particular one being owned by David Crosby of Crosby, Stills & Nash. Unfortunately, David couldn't be at the show due to being in prison for some misdemeanour or other. I would have dearly loved to have met the legend.

On this tour, there were a number of incidents, some reported with a tinge of 'Aye right, no' too bad mate!' In New York, we just about diverted disaster. Charlie had taken acid, and his trip was a bad one that lasted for well over two days. We had arrived in New York and were booked into the Hotel St. Moritz on Central Park South. Charlie was suffering as he was coming down. Jim and I were in his room watching over him in case he tried to do something stupid. He had been ranting about jumping out of the window. Not on our watch: we put Charlie in his bed, and lay either side of him on top of the covers, to keep him safe until morning. We never had much, if any sleep, but at least Charlie was back to his normal cheerful self and still with us in the morning.

A few days later, we're back in Toronto, at Massey Hall, a grand old hall. We were in the dressing room after soundcheck and who should come in to see us? None other than our legendary friend Peter Gabriel. He was playing the Maple Leaf Gardens and just popped in for a cup of tea and a fairy cake. It was great to see him again.

Two nights of Canadian madness and then on to be the first to play La Paladium in Montreal. The French-Canadian capital was always fantastic to play. Last time we played here was at Le Spectrum and the weather was the usual 35 degrees below. Luckily this time it was summer. We had a few days to enjoy the city before leaving for the Big Apple.

On 15 May we were back in New York, playing the Ritz. We arrived and the sound heck was complete. We did our check, playing 'The Sash My Father Wore' as per usual. Our sound man, Francis Xavier Gallagher, would respond by singing Celtic songs at me through the monitor while we were onstage playing the gig. If Mick was too loud, Gallagher would speak to him through the monitor – 'Morag … you're too loud' – then I would get, 'Hun … you're oot the mix!'

It was showtime at the Ritz. Before we started we were told that there was a very special guest in the audience. The intro music started, the smoke was pouring over the stage, lights were flashing, and we walked between two stage risers on our way to our instruments. I was second to go on and never saw the lighting cable in front of me. As I went forward, I tripped through the smoke and almost fell face first onto the stage floor, but managed to hold it – pure comedy for everyone, and pure embarrassment for me. As I looked up at the audience through the smoke I saw Olivia Newton-John looking back at us. I felt an absolute tit, and I just froze on the spot. The words 'what a fuckin' arsehole' echoed in my head for the whole show. When the gig was over, we went back to the dressing room. Jim wanted a post-mortem, so we sat for an hour before leaving the room, but unfortunately we didn't know that Olivia was waiting outside too, and had left minutes before we opened the door. The upside was that we heard the tape recording of the show, and it was perfect. The downside was I never met Olivia.

We were now going back to Britain to ready ourselves for festivals. The Pinkpop festival was in 8 days' time, and we needed to be fresh. I have vivid memories of playing Pinkpop. We wore our new Armani clothes from a shoot for Italian *Vogue*. We'd looked more like the Bash Street Kids or the Bowery Boys, than models. The clothes were fantastic and free, though, the best kind!

On the day of the gig in Geleen, Netherlands, we had a line check before heading back to the dressing room. There were a lot of acts on before us, so we lazed around a bit. John Peel came backstage and asked if we would like a kickabout before the show. So, we formed a couple of teams and ran about like madmen with the world-famous Liverpool supporter. It was a really sunny day, and the crowd were up for it. You can find footage online if you wish to see us. We had a ball!

The next gig wasn't until 24 June, where we played at the Paradiso in Amsterdam. I remember staying at the American Hotel for the first time. We were now entering the realms of Billy Big Time. Gone were the days of eating mushrooms off the back of the toilet door. We had a few days wandering around good old Amsterdam. There were women knitting underpants in the windows which glowed red in the night or were they sitting in their underpants knitting?

It's 1 July and we are now at the Roskilde Festival in Denmark. We played 'Street Hassle' for the first time live that night. The song had long been a favourite of the band, since sharing a label with Lou Reed at Arista Records. We would often play it at soundchecks, but now we decided to record it for the album. It worked well, but the original is something else. Danish audiences were magnificent to us.

It's 2 July, and a real change is coming. Our first gig at Torhout in Belgium puts us on the same stage as U2 for the first time, along with Peter Gabriel. There was a toss of a coin to see who went on second, Simple Minds or U2? We were second, which meant we had the chance to watch U2 in action – and they were staggeringly good, the best band I had ever seen at that time. Bono was climbing all over the stage, on the PA, he covered every inch of the stage like a wee cheeky monkey. It was now our turn to go on, and we played, trying to be cool as fuck and mysterious, not a lot of jumping around. I believe U2 were impressed. We hung out backstage after our show, going out only to watch Peter in action.

I met an old drummer of mine at the gate trying to get in. It was Jim Beveridge, wee Bev. We were at college together in Glasgow and he was a drummer. He joined the band I was forming then. I remember that my brother had given me some tabs of acid, and Bev was the only guy willing to take them with me. He dropped two or three tabs and was tripping out of his head. What were we like back then? I took wee Bev to meet Peter Gabriel, then U2 and our band. Wee Bev is no longer with us. He was a real character and I sorely miss him.

After the show we drove back to Brussels and we were staying at the Holiday Inn. I hung about with U2's Adam Clayton, who became a good friend. We were doing Rock & Roll things in between bottles of Dom Perignon. The next day we were playing the twin festival Werchter. It was always that way, Torhout and Werchter together, never alone. This time we went on before U2, and there was a subtle change to our performance. We moved about more, trying to own the stage more, a direct result of watching our new pals, and how they did it. When U2 came on, they didn't jump about as much, again as a direct homage to our way of doing things. Suddenly the press came up with a new moniker for us, U3, which died out after a month or two. After this, Bono would come on with us at various gigs, and Jim would reciprocate. One of our back-room team remarked, 'How good would we be with that chap singing?'

Back to Brussels and more madness. The morning after, we left Belgium for Italy. On 6 July we played Teatro Tenda in Rome. The venue, as in the name, was a theatre tent. These held about 7,000 people and the Romans were totally wild that night. Fights broke out, and there was a rush to the front of the stage. All very exciting, but a tad scary.

Next, it was time to play Tursport in Taranto. This gig was memorable not just for the show itself, but afterwards when we were leaving the stadium: crowds were waiting, and we had to drive through them. Our limo was covered in fans, all wanting to be close to us. It was claustrophobic but flattering all the same. On the 8th we were in Turin, had a night off and then headed to Bologna, a real stronghold of Simple Minds. The Italians had fallen in love with us, and we with them.

On the 11 July, we sailed to Sicily to play at the Palasport in Messina. Now we are in the town of Taormina, where Jim will have a share in a hotel in the future. Who would have known that Jim (and Charlie) would end up both living in Taormina – and on the same street. To be fair the whole band were besotted by Taormina, not just Jim and wee Charlie. It was our first gig on the Island, and we were bewitched by its beauty. Messina was chaotic and lots of people asked for our autographs, and photos, with proper cameras (no mobile phones in the '80s). There were lots of wooden puppets of knights hanging from walls and windows. I never found out why! The gig was open air and very hot. The crowd were passionate, and our wee Charlie could already speak a fair amount of Italian, in his inimitable Glaswegian way.

After the show we were up for a party. Many drinks later, and a few bottles of Zibibbo Sicilian white wine later, we staggered to our spinning beds and bid ciao to everyone. Morning came and went and we started to leave our rooms and meet up in the breakfast room, but obviously too late for a bit of breakfast. Being Rock & Roll soldiers, though, we were fit again in no time and went for a walk around the streets. Charlie, Mick and I booked a table for lunch al fresco overlooking the bay. We drank our wine and watched a local festival pass by. It was wonderful.

We drove to the ferry and sailed back to mainland Italy. To see the world, stay in the best hotels, eat at the best restaurants, meet lots of interesting people, travel in style, buy a cabbage in London at four in the morning and get paid – this is life on tour, and it's not bad.

The next day we drove to France heading for Toulouse for the Elixir Festival. It was a great bill, including King Sunny Adé, the Belle Stars, the Undertones, Joe Cocker, the Stranglers, and Aswad. The festival manager is our old friend Pascal, a tough Mohican Frenchman who carries an enormous machete around, hanging from his belt. King Sunny Adé had an enormous band. As he came onstage, he was accompanied by faint tribal singing which gradually became louder and louder until the stage was filled with what seemed like a hundred people, but was probably nearer forty. They played Highlife music which I loved. I chatted with the girls from Belle Stars. I watched a couple of the guys from Aswad playing tennis at the tennis courts backstage. They were awful and were suitably ganged out of their gourd. The Undertones were brilliant onstage. The love children of the late John Peel, they worked up the crowd to a frenzy with Feargal's wobbly vocals. He said to me, after the show, 'How can you tell ET is a Protestant?' 'How?' I said. 'Because he looks like one.' I said, 'You can fuckin' talk.' We laughed and carried on.

Afterwards we got packed up and were taken to a small airport. There were two planes waiting to take us north to Guéhenno in Brittany. We had to get ourselves up to Elixir Festival part two. Pascal took charge of the flight and boarding. I waved Joe Cocker off because he was on a different small plane. We were seated right behind Aswad, and across from us were the Belle Stars. The Undertones were a bit further forward. Pascal sat in the middle facing everyone like the Last of the Mohicans. We took off, and the boys from Aswad sparked up huge doobies; the plane smelled like Jamaica on a bank holiday. Pascal had a silver tray on his lap and began to chop out huge rails of wide-awake dust. We were asked collectively to raise our hand if we required powdery sustenance. Everyone did. One person went up, took a line. The second person went up, took a line, third person approached Pascal but stopped as the captain over the intercom asked us to all keep seated as we were wobbling the plane too much. He suggested the stewardess serve. And so, the poor lady had to go through the cabin dishing it out on a silver platter. We landed at a private airfield and disembarked. Buses were provided and we made our way to the festival backstage area. When we got there, the Stranglers were halfway through their set; brilliant as always. We hadn't seen them since supporting them in Aberdeen at Robert Gordon University. I watched the Belle Stars again, and they were fun. If the reaction from this huge crowd was anything to go by, you could say that Simple Minds had been greatly embraced by the French.

Our gigs now finished, we headed back to dear old Blighty for some songwriting time. There were supposed to be gigs in the USA and Canada with the Police but they never happened. Charlie and Mick went to a studio in London to work on some ideas and would call on me later. I was in Glasgow, working away on songs myself, and I came up with probably the most recognised Simple Minds song, starting with one note.

'Waterfront'

'Waterfront' was born in a bedroom at 46 Westbourne Gardens, Glasgow. Charlie and Mick were in London. So was Jim. I had a small Dynacord bass combo amplifier in my girlfriend's flat. It had a 1.5 second sampler on it. I played around with it, and soon managed to record the first two notes, which played back over and over. I was using my fretless Wal bass, and listened to the bass pulse, working out what to play on top of the line in my head. That was the string melody. I then put on slap bass as a percussive rhythm. Add to that the harmonics and stabs, which totals 4 or 5 parts on top of the constant bass pulse. That was how the music was written.

Cue a quote from Jim that makes me laugh: 'I think it's a great piece of music, I can say this because I wasn't involved in the music.' It begs the question, were you ever? The music came solely from Mick, Charlie and me, and whoever the drummer was. Jim was great lyrically but couldn't play a comb and a bit of paper. There are lots of amazing lyrics in his early work, but without the music his words could have been judged just average poetry. Having said that, I always liked Jim's lyrics right from the start. 'Seeing Out the Angel' for one, 'Pleasantly Disturbed' another; lots of his work was interesting and thought-provoking. Jim wasn't an amazing singer, but he was a great performer. He was the most difficult singer I have ever worked with for singing backing vocals, as he never sung the same melody twice.

We were five different elements that were brought together to make a whole, creating an incredible sound. I spoke to Mick MacNeil the other night, and he said that without any one of us, we might not have got so far in our careers, and I believe that to be right.

We were off to Nomis Studios in London when I bumped into Tina Turner. She gave me such a big smile as she passed me. I greeted her with 'Your Majesty', and she laughed. After that I bumped into the ubiquitous Lemmy Kilmister, he of Motörhead fame, for what must have been about the fifth or sixth time. Don't you love bumping into people?

At the end of the day, after listening to new ideas, the band started to pack up because were travelling to Dublin the next morning for the special guest slot at Phoenix Park with our new pals, U2. Before we left the studios, I began to play the pulse and the melodies for 'Waterfront'. Jim Kerr turned to me and asked what I was playing. I told him it was a piece of music that I had worked on at home. He then asked Mel to play along with me, then Charlie and Mick joined in, asking what my melody was and which key it was in. Within ten to fifteen minutes, we had the structure settled and all we needed was Jim to do his vocal bit, which he did. Between then and going on stage the next day in Ireland, 'Waterfront' was born – and the rest is history.

We started our show in Dublin with 'Waterfront', and then rattled through a great set. We were guests of U2 and therefore giving it our all. The Irish crowd loved the new song and jumped and bumped along to the rhythm. After the gig we watched U2 till the end, then we went off for a drink at Jurys Inn. Jim got a lift on the back of Bono's motorbike, in the pouring rain, and the rest of us travelled back in the limo with Ali, Bono's wife. When we got to the hotel the Guinness was being handed out. There is nowhere better in the world to have a pint of Guinness than Ireland. We pulled tables together and I remember Peter O'Toole was sitting with us, and Errol Brown of Hot Chocolate. He was bald as a coot, so much so that young Mark Kerr shouted over to him, 'Hey mate, can I borrow your comb?' What a great night that was.

September 1983, we make the trip to Monnow Valley Studio at Rockfield, again in Wales. We are heading there to do some songwriting for a couple of weeks. Steve Lillywhite will accompany us for the latter stage of the writing, so that we can begin arranging what we have come up with. This is the early stages of what will become the album *Sparkle in the Rain*. We already have an early take of 'Waterfront', so now we just need to polish it before the final recording. These weeks had an intense feel; maybe the album had to be different in feel and sound to our classic *New Gold Dream* album. It certainly was a new experience working with Steve Lillywhite.

I sat my first UK driving test there and the man who took me for the test looked exactly like my old college teacher, who hated me. I thought, 'I bet he fails me!' And the old, speccy git did. I then let him know that I had passed my test in Hollywood and that I could legally drive for a year in the UK. His face dropped as I jumped out of the car, but I resisted giving him the bird.

We rolled out of old Rockfield and headed for Shepherd's Bush, London, to start recording the album properly. I remember John Martyn, an amazing musician, staying in the rooms above the studio. He was like our big brother. One night we stayed up recording for 24 hours, helped by a big slab of hash. I was buzzing. On the day we recorded 'The Kick

Inside of Me', we had a visit from U2's manager, Paul McGuinness. He sat and chatted with our manager Bruce Findlay, as they were now very good friends. Steve Lillywhite asked if we could have a bit of hush. He was ready to record my bass part, from inside the control room. I tuned up and Steve got the sound up. Off we went. I was slapping my bass part like a demon, and towards the end my thumb burst open, spraying blood all over the place, but soldier that I am, I didn't stop, or miss a beat. I made it to the end of the track, and we played it back. It was perfect. Paul McGuinness turned to me and said my performance was amazing, then named me 'The Once and Future King.' That was the last bass line of the album, and I was finished.

I was sent up to Glasgow to check out if the Barrowland music venue would be suitable for us to play. I flew to Glasgow and went over to the Barrowland to see what it was like and whether it could re-open for us. I couldn't believe how big it was. It could have easily held four thousand people. It was up to me whether we should go there. Of course, I said yes! And we started to form a plan to use it as soon as humanly possible. Our crew – headed by my favourite Kerr, Paul – put together a big stage to perform on by borrowing lots of smaller stages from venues all over Britain, and they are still there today.

At the end of October, the album is finished. In November 'Waterfront' is released, and it charts, so much so that we appear on *Top of the Pops* again. We arranged a gig in which we would unveil 'Waterfront' to a live Glasgow audience at the newly reopened Barrowland. We filmed the concert in front of hundreds of fans and then played gigs at Barrowland several times more in December. Two videos were filmed there, 'Waterfront' and 'Speed Your Love to Me', and now the latter had been released and had charted at Number 20. Virgin Canada had released a promo album, *Sparkle Through the Years*, as a precursor to the real thing.

We were delighted with the gigs at the end of last year, and the highlight for me was being honoured with the responsibility of giving the thumbs up for the reopening of Glasgow's Barrowland Ballroom, and I was awarded a plaque for services to the venue.

6. Once More into the Breeks

Before I continue with the story, let's have a quick recap. So, 1984 started as the best year ever for me and for Simple Minds but finished rather abruptly for me. I was sacked! No longer with my mates and no longer on tour, I retreated to my farmhouse, Craigmarloch, in Kilmacolm.

In the meantime, I kept myself busy on the farm. I made a deal with one of the local farmers, agreeing to let him put some 'beasts' (cattle) on my land, and I housed a few horses for some local riders. I let the people from the hunt know that they could not ride through my land chasing foxes, which they honoured. I rescued a deer that had been knocked down by a car, and I slept most of the night with it in one of my stables, keeping guard from anyone who might fancy a bit of venison.

It was at this time I met Andy Christie and his wife Gaye, of Hessilhead Wildlife Rescue Centre, and I would do a lot of work for them in my spare time, picking up injured animals from various locations in Scotland. Swans were a good pant filler if you believed the old fairy tale about them breaking people's arms with a blow from their wings.

I received a call from an old musician friend of mine, Ray McVeigh. I had been introduced to him by my pal, Richard Jobson, and we became firm friends. Ray came up to see me at home and we had a great weekend writing songs – 23 in total in one weekend. I went to London to see him the next week, and we went to the house of Ultravox legend, Billy Currie, to let him hear some of the tracks. Billy liked what he heard, and we made plans to go back to Craigmarloch the next weekend to record some demos and write some more. We also invited Ray Weston, the drummer extraordinaire, to put in his tuppence-worth.

After a hard day's shift in the music room, we broke for dinner. Afterwards we decided to have a swim and sauna. I fired up the sauna, and Billy went in first, wearing his underpants, and I think Ray went next, to find Billy smoking as he lay there … put it out, put it out, you'll cause a fire! Billy was hilarious and kept the laughs coming with his dry sense of humour. Ray Weston went into the sauna and lay on the top bench. He

Derek Forbes

Ray McVeigh and Mick MacNeil

fell asleep, and Ray McVeigh joined him in there. He poured water on the coals and nearly scalded the drummer. We laughed, drank, smoked and made merry. Certainly helped me after leaving Simple Minds. We agreed to resume the next week at Billy's studio. One track we recorded was called 'India', which ended up on Billy's solo album.

I had a call from Virgin Records. They wanted me to record some demos, and they booked me into the Virgin Barge in London. Ray, Billy Currie, Geordie Walker of Killing Joke and I turned up at the studios to put down some tracks. Geordie is a legendary guitar player, and he was great that day. We have kept in touch ever since that day, and I have seen Killing Joke a few times. The engineer at the studio was a little French chap called François. I remember a point where he missed a good guitar take from Geordie, who whacked him across the ear. Mayhem ensued, but the end result was fine to our ears. However, Virgin weren't playing ball this time.

It was back to the farm for me, and it was then that I started horse riding on a daily basis. I wasn't the most confident of riders at that point, but as the weeks passed my riding and jumping got much better. I had an offer to go play on an album with Frida from ABBA around that time, but Bruce Findlay also called me and told me he had spoken with Keith Bourton, our old press officer at Virgin Records. Bourton was

Once More into the Breeks

Derek, and Raven from Killing Joke in Malibu, California

now managing bands such as Heaven 17, Swing Out Sister and PIL, to name but three, as well as a German band called Propaganda, from Düsseldorf. He wanted to know if I would play with them for two weeks at the Ambassador Theatre in Soho for a spectacular for ZTT Records, to be filmed by Godley & Creme, the 10cc legends. I asked who else would be playing, and he said the German band and Steve Jansen from Japan on drums. *Wow*, thought I, *he's great*. I agreed and I began my seven-year tenure with the band. Frida would have to wait.

Propaganda

Steve Jansen and I got on famously and would take a trip to the studio to hear the band recording their new album. I was still so stunned and shocked at now being an ex-member of Simple Minds, and being sacked. Over time that would change; my darkness was beginning to crack, and the light was breaking through. My whole involvement with Propaganda was masterminded by my best school friend, Ian Reekie; it was he who raved to me about this new German band and their single 'Dr. Mabuse', which he had heard on the radio. My decision to say yes was his, not mine. At this time, we were going into rehearsals for the ZTT shows at the Ambassador.

Meeting the Propaganda band was a great experience. Every member of the band could speak English, and my German was sporadic, but not too bad. It didn't take long for the band to supply me with phrases, some polite and some outrageous. The first shows with Propaganda were in London; we did 14 in all. Steve and I loved to mimic Claudia Brücken's voice. Her voice, a bit like Kermit the Frog, was distinct. It fitted the band perfectly. Every time Steve and I entered the dressing room we would belt out the lyric 'on joyless lanes, we walk in line, a calm but steady flow …' Sometimes Claudia would catch us, sometimes not, but it soon became routine. The gigs were great. Steve and I would often go to a Japanese restaurant–dining club not far from the theatre, and drink cocktails. Steve would sit at the bar spinning a coin through his fingers like a modern-day George Raft. The ladies were mesmerised. Who was this young Elvis Presley double sitting at the bar? We had a great laugh in those days. On the opening night of the ZTT shows, Jim Kerr came to the show. I can't remember speaking to him, but maybe I did.

Propaganda, Derek, Brian, Betsi and Mich

Susanne Freytag was lovely, with an incredible sounding voice. Ralf Dörper was a big character. He is the only man who can play keyboards with boxing gloves on, and it still sounds note perfect. Claudia laughed a lot, sang a lot, and had a very striking look. Michael Mertens was the genius behind the band, a trained musician and a wonderful songwriter in partnership with Ralf. It was an honour for me to spend seven years with the band. I learned so much, from Michael especially. After the London Shows we made a trip to Carlisle to Border TV Studios, where Janet Street-Porter had us on her music show, *Bliss*. This was to be the last time Steve Jansen played with the band; he left soon after to join up with keyboard player Richard Barbieri, from Japan, and form the Dolphin Brothers. Steve came up to my farm just before we played the show. We played some tunes on my boudoir grand piano, which I loved. Steve played the theme from *Merry Christmas, Mr. Lawrence* – and I must say, the boy could play. I was sad to see Steve go. It was great getting to know and befriend him. An astounding drummer, and cool as fuck. We needed to find a suitable replacement.

My old ex-Simple Minds mate, Brian McGee, and I had started playing five-a-side football together, and one night he was at my house, no doubt poncing some hash from me. We sat upstairs in the living room, smoking our brains out, when I asked him if he fancied playing drums with Propaganda. He immediately said yes: he had recently stopped playing with Endgames and was at a loose end. A big world tour was coming up, taking in the UK, Europe, Japan, America and Canada, and our rehearsals would soon be starting in London. The band welcomed Brian with open arms, and also recruited the wonderful Kevin Armstrong on guitar and a Teac on incidentals and keyboards. Ralf never came on the tour. In the interim Propaganda had been touring television and radio stations all over the globe. They also made a video for 'p:Machinery' in New York. We played *The Old Grey Whistle Test* and the very last gig with Claudia Brücken too around this time.

At the end of 1985 we played *The Tube*. This was the end of live performances for Propaganda, but what a great end! Susanne and Claudia looked incredible in copies of 1930s' Kempinski dresses (think *Cabaret*). The girls had worked out a great routine for the song 'Frozen Faces', and it stands up to this day as their best performance ever, in my eyes.

One night after rehearsals Kevin Armstrong, our guitar player, said to me that he had a meeting with Bowie and Jagger in Soho at an all-night diner in Greek Street at 4 a.m. This was the birth of the two superstars performing 'Dancing in the Street' for Live Aid, and Kevin was the musical director. Kevin went on to play at Live Aid in David Bowie's band, and then had years of guitar work with Iggy Pop.

Propaganda stayed regularly at Craigmarloch for two years on and off. I would go to Michael's house in Düsseldorf for three months, where we would write songs. We also spent a lot of time at Skyline, Peter Krick's studio, where we met up with the former superstar Bodo and Der Falsche Heino. There were also mornings when we had breakfast with the musician Karl Bartos of Kraftwerk, a veritable hero. We spent evenings clubbing, and would often see Ralf Hütter, yet another of the Kraftwerk Four. The whole experience was surreal.

One day Karl took us to Kraftwerk's studio, which had at least four identical set-ups of keyboards and electronic gadgetry and recording equipment. The weirdest thing was the location – a wartime Gestapo building near the centre of Düsseldorf.

I felt that things were going well for me at this time. When the original band were staying at my house at Craigmarloch, I would let them go out riding with my horse Blue Bayou. On a weekend off, I met up with the Simple Minds crew of Brian McGee, Mick MacNeil, Charlie Burchill and Jim and we drove to Balloch at Loch Lomond to go out on Captain Jim Kerr's boat for a jolly time, pirating and schmoking reefer. It was just us, and nobody else. All pals, all Simple Minds once again, having fun. It was a fantastic, nostalgic day. I have footage of it somewhere. At one point, Captain Jim lad grounded the vessel on a sandbank. Pirate McGee and me jumped overboard and pushed her off the bank and scrambled back on, and successfully set sail again. Years later I would buy a boat which I moored there, but only went out on her once. What a plonker!

I had a two-year break from Propaganda while they sorted out a contract issue and this gave me a lot of spare time. I went into the studio with my best female friend, Kirsty MacColl, to record bass on her version of Billy Bragg's 'A New England'. It became a hit for Kirsty, and it was a pleasure to record with her. Kirsty was a great friend, and a genius. We originally met when she was introduced to me by my pal Ray McVeigh, and she smoked the same brand of head smoke as the band and me. I introduced Kirsty to our then producer, Steve Lillywhite, and someone must have sprinkled fairy dust because they fell in love shortly after meeting. Wedding bells were in the air, and I was to be their best man, but couldn't make it because Simple Minds, at that time, were off to tour America. The things we do!

In 1987, Propaganda were now free from their restrictive recording contract with ZTT. Frankie Goes to Hollywood had successfully managed to get out of an identical contract, and this led the way for Propaganda to do the same. At last, we could pursue interested parties in the recording world. Claudia Brücken had left the band and we had recruited a new singer, Betsi Miller. Betsi was an army brat from Boise, Idaho, USA, and spoke perfect German, which was perfect for the band – and she could sing. Betsi also had striking features and suited the image of the band. We toured London, speaking to various record companies, Virgin, CBS, London Records, Polydor, etc. We had a meeting with the MD of Polydor Records, and as the meeting came to an end, the boss man said, 'Do you mind if I smoke?', to which Betsi quickly replied, 'Do you mind if I fart?' We fell about laughing, and as we left, I turned to him and said, 'I couldn't eat another thing' – to point out the lack of tea, biscuits … goodbye Polydor. In the end Virgin gave us the best offer, and so we signed – me for the second time, and Brian McGee for the third time.

Around this time, and since I had been sacked by Simple Minds, I would go out to bars and clubbing with Charlie Burchill. We would head into the West End of Glasgow most weekends if we were both in town. My brother, John, had laid a lovely new floor for me, and I remember Charlie saying that he would like to pay for it because he walked across my floor every time he came to my house. I thanked him for his kind offer but said no thanks. Charlie, as said before, felt really bad that I'd been asked to leave the band, and he tried for years to convince Jim to take me back, but to no avail.

By this time Propaganda were preparing to travel down to Bath to start the new album with producers Ian Stanley and Chris Hughes. Before we left Scotland, we went to see U2 at the SECC and at the end of the show Adam Clayton came back to party on at Craigmarloch. Betsi had a wee shine for him. Adam and I played bass and guitar in my music room; he was so merry that he couldn't tune the bass, but then again, why would he need to? He liked my Vigier bass, so I gave him it to keep. In exchange for the bass, Adam gave me a bottle of Dom Perignon, which he put into my big chest freezer. Of course, we were so stoned and out of our faces that we forgot about it and the bottle exploded.

Charlie Burchill was still coming to my house so that we could go into Glasgow for a night out. I had been going out with a girl who worked for Radio Clyde as a news reporter. One night when we were in Glasgow, we went to the Cul de Sac in Ashton Lane. It was a late summer's evening. She introduced me to a stunning girl with mad hair, who worked behind the bar. I was smitten and chatted to her for a short time before leaving for a club. I couldn't get her out of my mind.

Charlie and I went into town the next week, and before I left, I went on the tanning bed. After trawling some of the bars, Charlie and I ended up in the Sub Club. Lo and behold, the same girl was working a second job. As we were leaving, she came out. I was going to ask if she would like to go for dinner sometime, but I blew it: I asked her if she fancied coming back to my house. She said, 'No, I don't do that sort of thing on a chance meeting, but I will give you my phone number and you can call me tomorrow if you are serious.' We parted, and Charlie and I went away to a friend's house in town. I was starting to hallucinate, as I had given myself sunstroke from my tanning bed at home. Wow, was I feeling ill. I got to the farm in the small hours of Saturday morning with Charlie. He left in the morning, and I started my recovery. On Saturday night, I was compos mentis enough to phone this girl and invite her out for dinner in my home village in Kilmacolm on Sunday. I was delighted when she said yes, and I drove into Glasgow to her flat in Sauchiehall Street, with my white BMW 323i, hoping to impress, to pick her up.

Her name is Wendy Kemp. She was born in Australia at the same hospital as another petite Aussie, Kylie, in Melbourne. I knew Melbourne well. Wendy's dad, Roy Kemp, was a professional football player who played for Scotland (Under-23) with Jimmy Johnstone and Martin Ferguson (Sir Alex's brother). In Scotland, he played for Falkirk and St. Mirren. He was sent down to Blackpool and was trained by Sir Stanley Matthews as a 17-year-old. Later, he played for Carlisle United and then a spell with the Welsh wizards, Rhyl FC. Roy had a leg break against Hearts, and when it mended, he decided to take a footballing job in Australia for Croatia (Melbourne Knights FC). Wendy was born, and not too long after the family moved back to Glasgow.

Getting Married

I was in Bath for one year at Woolhall Studios, recording the second album *1234* with Propaganda. I would drive down from Scotland on a

Monday morning with Brian McGee, and we would drive back up on a Friday. It was a week after meeting Wendy that I asked her to marry me, and on 22 April 1988 we were an item. Simple Minds came to the wedding with the management team, and the management team from Propaganda were there too, Mathew Stumpf and Mike Collins. Kirsty MacColl and Steve Lillywhite were also there, and Billy Currie from Ultravox. Charlie had taken me out to a great antique store in my area to show me what the band had bought us as a wedding present. It was a great big antique kitchen store cupboard, and it was stunning. The miserable bastards never gave us it in the end! Paul and Valerie Kerr gave us some beautiful pottery, and a big matching plate. Bruce Findlay and Jane gave us more of the same.

Propaganda was a class outfit. They got us an antique sculpture of a Napoleonic general on a horse, which we still have. Everyone was dressed in their finest, and one man stood out like a sore thumb. He was resplendent in a two-piece denim jacket and jeans, and long unwashed hair. Of course, he was the old rock and roll Dr. Robert with the 'stuff', which sold out in no time.

Sharyn Kemp, Wendy Kemp Forbes, Derek Forbes, John Henry Forbes

Wedding guests, Jimmy Devlin, Charlie, Ralf Dörper, Kirsty MacColl and friends

At the actual wedding, my horse groom, Chandler Dallas Gray, rode to the church on my horse, and our dog Kinski was at the house with one of my raccoons. It was all a bit Doctor Dolittle. At the end of our honeymoon, I got the call to pick up a deer that was stuck on my doctor's fence. I was to take it to Hessilhead animal sanctuary. So, Wendy and I went over to the doctor's, picked up the distressed deer, and put her into the back seat of my BMW. We drove to the sanctuary and could see a camera team at the bottom of the road. Standing there, larger than life, was David Bellamy and a BBC crew. He remarked that this was the first time he had ever seen a deer get out of a BMW. He was a lovely man. His wife had accompanied him and she too was a gem. They also kept raccoons. As for the deer, she had contracted pneumonia and never lasted the night, poor thing.

Brian McGee and I continued our drives to Bath, Monday to Friday. Our producers – Ian Stanley of Tears for Fears and Chris Hughes of Adam and the Ants – would determine how long our journeys were each week, measuring by the number of joints we smoked. 'Oh, that was a nine joint journey, and last week it was only seven.'

Time passed and on 1 November 1988 our first son, Kai, was born. Wendy's labour started on the Friday, and we were moving house on the Saturday! Wendy stayed with her cousin, Sandra, before we took her to hospital. Meanwhile, I said goodbye to my lovely farm, and began the move to Strathaven, a *Hills Have Eyes*-style village south of Glasgow. It was a beautiful millhouse with a waterfall which belonged to us, Powmillion Falls. But before Wendy and Kai came to the house, I had decided that it was the wrong move, and we were now looking for houses in Pollokshields. Around the same time, I started talking about the possibility of me returning to Simple Minds.

Almost Back with Simple Minds

In December 1988 I was invited up to Bonnie Wee Studio to listen to the new Simple Minds album, with the view to having me return to the band as a writer and player. They offered me a great wage, even by today's standards. The album was *Street Fighting Years* and Jim took me into the studio and played it to me. My one desire at that time was to be back in the band, touring, writing, and playing, but the songs I was hearing left me cold. I just didn't like them. I spoke to Wendy, and she was nervous at the thought of being left at home with a one-year-old on her own without me. So I decided not to rejoin.

We had been living in Strathaven for six months and had now put an offer in for a lovely house with a big garden in Pollokshields. This was to be our home for the next ten years. I had a great studio installed, and I was to do lots of work there over the years. I worked with the BBC comedy unit, where I would record my pal Jonathan Watson for *Only an*

Derek with his son Kai

Excuse and provide music for his sketches in the theatre too. It was great work, and very enjoyable.

I also did an album for my team, Glasgow Rangers, and had most of the first team in my house to sing some choruses. I was invited to Ally McCoists's testimonial game at Ibrox, which led to me being invited on a trip to Toronto with Rangers for Ally's testimonial dinner, and Ian Durrant's stag night. What a week that was! I then played at Ian Durrant's testimonial at Ibrox. When I was introduced as Derek Forbes of Simple Minds to the huge crowd, they wanted to lynch me, obviously not knowing that I was a Rangers fan. Lots of people were mumbling, proclaiming that I was one of them, which helped.

If this book was solely about football we would be here forever, but more about the music. Propaganda, by this time, were working in Abbey Road in Paul McCartney's private studio in the attic. We had Greg Hawkes of the Cars playing keyboards for us on some tracks, and another amazing coup for us was having Dave Gilmour playing a guitar solo on one of our tracks, 'Only One Word'. What an interesting man and an incredibly kind philanthropist.

7. Simple Minds, Take Two

I got a call from Charlie Burchill saying that Simple Minds wanted me back, and that he had convinced Jim Kerr it was the right thing to do. I knew Charlie had been fighting my corner for a long time, but I thought, *why should I go back?* So, I told him that I was going to stick with Propaganda, although I never earned a penny from them. I had worked at Abbey Road for six and a half months and loved every minute of it. One day, the phone rang at the Studio. It was John Leckie, who was in Studio 2 with the Stone Roses, recording their first album. The band had run out of personality cigarettes, and did we have some? We took them downstairs and gave them to the band. I think it was 'Waterfall' that was playing in the background.

Propaganda moved into Olympic Studios, Red Dog Studios and the Townhouse Studios until the album was eventually finished. I went with Betsi Miller on a promotional tour all over Europe, and Brian went with Michael Mertens to other northernly climes. We covered a lot of ground, including the Sopot Festival in Gdańsk, Poland.

At the airport on our way home, I treated everybody to macaroni and cheese. It cost me 13 pence in total for the four of us! Later, when we were back in Germany, the decision was made that the Props would not tour anymore. Michael said that he was going to have to sack Brian, so I told Michael that if Brian was out, then I had to go as well. And so, we parted.

Back home in Scotland again, my second son, Dylan Kemp Forbes, was born, on 7 December 1994. When he was six weeks old, I left on a tour of Europe and the UK with my great mate, Kirk Brandon, in his new band 10:51. Kirk, Ray McVeigh, Pete Barnacle and I had been working on a new venture. There had been some great songs that were not destined to see the light until much later.

I had a call from the Simple Minds office with a request from Jim. He asked if I would escort his wife, Patsy Kensit, to a Rangers match for him. I agreed and took Patsy with me to Ibrox. What a commotion that made. Everyone – punters and players, staff and fans – were asking me

Saying goodbye

Simple Minds, Take Two

Wendy Kemp Forbes and Patsy Kensit

who my girlfriend was. I explained that it was my old workmate's wife, and she loved the Rangers. Patsy, Jim and I then arranged a night for dinner at the Rogano in Glasgow City Centre. Wendy and Patsy became great friends after that.

Back with Simple Minds

Many bottles of Cristal later and visits to our house, there was another phone call asking if I would go up to Bonnie Wee Studios to play bass on the latest album *Néapolis*. I was asked to pick up our old producer, Pete Walsh, from the airport. I drove us up north, through stunning Highland scenery and passing Jim's house, Ardchullerie. I spoke to Jim when we arrived, asking what my role was; he said the songs were almost finished and he wanted me to do my stuff on the bass.

I said, if I write a bass line, then that's co-written by me. He said no, we don't work like that anymore; we just want you as a session player. I said OK, you tell me what you want me to play.

Of course, they didn't. On 'Glitterball' Charlie played chords on the bass and strummed them throughout the song. It wasn't until we played the song live that it had any balls. It was just awful to begin with, but it grew on me when I punked it up some more.

Mariella Frostrup, Kai Forbes and Patsy Kensit, Bonnie Wee Studio

At night, one of us would drive for miles to get a takeaway – even as far as Stirling, if required. When fed, we would break out the Scrabble board and tiles, and the loser would have to stand up and sing a song of the winner's choice. Charlie very rarely loses at Scrabble. Pete and I were the main chorus line, probably myself more than those two chaps. It didn't bother me in the slightest, but Pete was a wee bit shy when it came to wiggling the tonsils. One night I had a strange omen from my seven tiles: 'ROB' and 'ROY' with a blank tile in the middle; that was exactly how the tiles came out!

During the mixing of the songs from *Néapolis*, things got a bit feisty at times. Charlie could be a wee angry man at times. I spent a lot of time on the bass and drums with Pete, and we worked out some iconic Minds parts, only to have them buried in the mix at the end of the album. Brian McGee had come up for the recording, but they never used him, which was a shame. They contacted Mel and got him to come up. We had a video to make for 'Glitterball' in Bilbao at the Guggenheim Museum. That was a fantastic trip – and the food and drink exceptional.

We ended up going to Dublin to rehearse for the Néapolis tour. Jim and Charlie both had houses there in Killiney. At the bottom of Charlie's garden there was a road, and then it was Bono's house. We would frequent the pub in Dalkey, with a dark corner near a fireplace there that we nicknamed Cauldron Corner. While I was in Ireland, my beautiful dog Kinski left us. She was the best.

There was a trip to Naples coming up, where we had the photoshoot for the album. My old flatmate, Linda Lawrence, was doing wardrobe for us, and Helen Wheels was doing make-up. One day we did a shoot in the middle of the road, with cars passing us by millimetres. Linda and I watched in amazement as a man, the spitting image of Geppetto from *Pinocchio*, drove by in a Fiat Uno, with a live donkey standing up on all fours in the back seat.

The next morning, we photographed at the ferry terminal and bus stops, and those are the shots on the album.

Back on Tour

There were now gigs coming up for us, and lots of television appearances. We performed all over Europe that year. It got to the point where we would all meet at Heathrow or Gatwick airport on a Thursday and get back home on the Monday.

First, we flew to a hotel in Antwerp, Belgium, where we set up in the basement. Rehearsals began and we ran through the set. At night, after we had slaved our way through the songs, we would go out for food and then the beer bars; Mel loved Belgian beer. We started rehearsals in the late morning.

Charlie started talking to me about recording set-ups, and asked what I was using. I told him that I don't get into the intricacies of the set-up, and that I prefer just to write music and record parts to play along with. He thought that was a bit stupid, and virtually said so. *Each to his own*, thought I, and we had a wee argument, daft boyness, where only egos were hurt.

I must admit, I did throw a pint of beer over our long-time roadie/boffin, Big Dougie, when he flicked a peanut at me which hit me on the nose. My reaction was swift, and the big man took a beer bath. Charlie left the room, fed up with the antics, and I followed him to apologize.

I have never been totally into the technicalities of the electronic side of music. I would rather just work with a groove, electronic or otherwise, and I prefer writing in my head, more than relying on a computer. Michael Mertens from Propaganda said that I put human soul into the songs.

We travelled back to London for a secret, invitation-only gig being filmed for *VH1* in Camden. It was on 11 February, and there were a host of special guests, and half of Toryglen. My old Liverpool Boys Club teammate, Willie Haughey, was there. And Matt Dunn. On St Valentine's Day we played with an orchestra in Rome, at an Amnesty International Concert. That was fun. More rehearsals and a wee trip on a Learjet for a TV show in Venice, then back to Antwerp for more rehearsals.

It was now May Day, or in Italian, Primo Maggio. We were to play this huge festival at Piazza San Giovanni – opening the show, then coming back on to close the show. The expected audience was 650,000 people. The day before we were approaching the runway in Rome, we were looking out of the window, just about to land, when our roadie, Jimmy Madden, spotted a plane right below us on the tarmac. With 20 seconds to spare the pilot shot up into the air, leaving a lot of people panic-stricken, especially the school children and the nuns in charge. We survived, but we couldn't help thinking that we had another four flights on this run, before we got home. Of course, the Italian press had a field day. Next day we were onstage waiting for our turn and at one point it began to rain; all the umbrellas sprang up like a field of cartoon flowers.

I had invited a family friend, from London and Malta: Romena Xicluna, Marquessa of Malta. I used to bow before her every time we met, and she would laugh it off and tell me to get up. After the show, Her Highness gave her approval. The gig had gone down extremely well. There were some huge Italian acts on with us, and a host of others, including Richie Sambora and Julian Lennon. After a bit of schmoozing, we retired to our hotel. We then had a bit of time off in Rome, and Mel, Mark Taylor and I went out with his friend, the dentist, and a couple of ladies who were friends of the dentist. The paparazzi had a field day. We were meeting up for dinner with the dentist and the ladies. There was, Mark Taylor (keyboard player for Simple Minds for this tour), Mel Gaynor and me. We sat waiting for the dentist and his ladies to arrive.

There was a sudden commotion and a loud gaggle of people arrived at the restaurant. It was Paul Young and his band. They were all shouty and having a ball. They came over to say hello to us, and all of a sudden, a limo turned up with the dentist and his ladies, who turned out to be escorts, and flashbulbs were going off like a crazy firework display. Loads of paparazzi surrounded us, but completely ignored Paul Young and his entourage.

We flew in and out of Europe at this time doing TV shows, but it was three weeks before we did another live show. On 22 May 1998 we played Festivalbar in Padova, Italy. Absolutely no recollection of this one, but it must have been a good night if I can't remember it. We rolled into Brussels to perform at the Cyber Theatre again on 25 May. The gig was as expected, but I remember talking to lots and lots of fans back at the hotel. We were interviewed by different magazines and radio people – it was great to get a chance to talk for a change. On the 28th, we were meant to be supporting the Rolling Stones in Zagreb, Croatia, but Keef fell off his ladder in his library at home and they had to cancel the gig. I had been really looking forward to it.

On 30 May we were at the Palasport, Pesaro, Italy. Palasport had a huge fence outside, with security people at every few feet. After the show we were driving through swarms of happy fans, wanting to rip the clothes off of us. Things were still a bit Beatle-like after all these years. Onwards my good man, and don't spare the horses …

We went to Sweden to play Karlshamn Festival, in early June. I went for a wander in the morning when we arrived, and found close to the hotel a museum examining torture from the Second World War. I heard a noise behind me and in walked Jim Kerr. We walked around the exhibits together in silence, not enjoying what we were seeing. In the afternoon we headed to the festival site, and got settled in, before having a line check.

The Swedes were great. The London show on 6 June had been cancelled, so we went to Germany the day before the Münster gig. I met up with Wendy in Düsseldorf and we had dinner with Michael Mertens. The next morning, we went to Düsseldorf Hauptbahnhof and boarded a train to Münster. We were going to meet the Dalai Lama. When we arrived, we missed him by minutes, we were late. Wendy has never forgiven me for that.

In June, we had a gig back in our favourite town of old, beautiful Bologna. The venue was Maggiore, in the centre of the city. It looked so good as night fell to darken the atmosphere and accentuate the huge lighting rig that we used.

Two days later, 16 June, we were in Barcelona, Spain. Luz de Gas, my old stomping ground of 1977. The next gigs were exceptional, and now we get to play two gigs with my personal heroes, the Rolling Stones. We were not a support act in our story, except the first couple of years with Magazine and then our other hero, Peter Gabriel – but these gigs were going to be extra special. Torhout and Werchter you already know about, but we were invited by the Stones as special guests. We booked into our hotel in Brussels and did a huge press conference before making our way to the first gig.

Fuck me! The backstage area was bigger than the gig area, and that had an audience of 72,000 people. There were trucks for miles, huge marquees for feeding the bands and the road crew. It looked like a small city. We were shown our huge dressing room, just off the Voodoo Lounge, which was like an enormous club with lots of fake animal skins on chairs and sofas, and whacky lighting. Food of all sorts was on offer as well as a wide range of alcohol, soft drinks, coffees and teas. Every table had packs of different types of cigarettes and cigars, chewing, gum, lighters, matches … just everything you could ever want.

The Stones came into the room with us to watch a World Cup game, USA v Iran. We were sitting there with Keef and Ronnie and, of course, Charlie Watts beside us, when Mick Jagger came in and stood beside the TV and said, 'What's the score?' And Ronnie Wood piped up 'Nuttin', nil.'

We walked onstage to great applause and we started with 'Waterfront'. At the back of the stage were massive screens for watching the band, and as soon as the first big line came in for Jim to sing, he leapt high into the air with excitement. His trousers around the arse region split wide open. Nor was he wearing the regulation clickers, so his tousled hair was poking out and magnified to an incredible size on the huge screens. Fuck me, I nearly choked with laughter. He managed to shuffle about, and someone gave him a jacket to tie around him for the rest of the gig – or did I imagine that part?

We came off and then walked to the VIP area to watch the Rolling Stones. On our way we passed Keef and Ronnie having a quick puff before going on. I must say Charlie Watts was one of the nicest people

I have ever met. He told me that all he wanted to do was tour, because that's where he made his fortune. He was a very down-to-earth man and a total musical legend.

We returned to our hotel in Brussels and so did the Stones, we were all staying in the same place.

The next day, 21 June, we did it all again. Then went back to the hotel again. The next morning, I said goodbye to Charlie Watts and the rest, and thanked them for having us.

After gigs in Belgrade, Vienna and Varsselder (The Netherlands), we travelled to Poland, one of the most beautiful places I have ever been. In Warsaw, we play Bowie's 'Warszawa' on the speakers. Next it's Budapest, Hungary, on the morning of 2 July. There's a big press conference before the soundcheck; we sit around together and are asked questions in English about the tour, the album, etc, but a couple of plants keep throwing in questions about how we like Pepsi Cola. Jim sussed out what they were doing pretty quickly, and basically told them to ask serious questions and just fuck off with the Pepsi ads.

We then had a day off, so Charlie and I went for a walk and a late lunch. We saw a commotion outside what looked like a pizza restaurant. There were camera crews and lights everywhere and lots of police and ambulances. We thought it was a film being made. It turned out to be a Mafia hit, and the place was in uproar. We just carried on as if nothing had happened, like the Glasgow boys we are, and found somewhere to eat.

After playing Midtyfns Festival in Copenhagen, Denmark, an addition to the tour, we were off on an overnighter to Ireland, for two gigs at the Olympia in Dublin. Wendy brought my youngest son, Dylan, to see me play, escorted by Eveline, my mother-in-law. We did all our checks and were ready for the show. Wendy and Eveline had Dylan between them in a private box right next to the stage. When we started, Dylan got such a fright from all the cheers. He began to cry at the sight of fans holding their arms out trying to shake my hand and screaming. It was cute, but he was distraught, so my mother-in-law took him to the dressing room to calm him down. Nowadays, 2023, he plays in his own band, Dr Veers, all over Britain, getting some of the same treatment. They really are very good. Dylan sings, plays guitar and bass, just like his old dad, and my other son Kai does the same, bass and guitar, and he is fantastic too, and very cool onstage.

The gig was mad, and the day after we played again, and it was just as mad. I do really like Dublin.

On 10 July we were now in Germany again, in Köln (Cologne). The gig was at the Kölner Dom, Roncalliplatz. The next gig was in Luxembourg on 11 July, and it was Bommelrock Festival, Bascharage. I must have been on acid for these last two gigs, as they have escaped my memory. Please feel free to fill in the blanks.

The next day of the tour, 12 July in Dunkirk, was cancelled but on the 13th, we did play Dunkirk, at Pas-de-Calais. I remember the gig. It looked like a massive drill hall. Everything was on the one level, apart from the raised stage. It was clad in lovely old wooden slats, and I cast my mind back to times of conflict and imagined the wounded lying here in a makeshift hospital, waiting for the fleet of little ships to take them back to Blighty. We played our hearts out that night, and I think that was with a nod to the young boys who weren't coming back on both sides; it certainly was for me.

On the 15th we played an amphitheatre at Château-Arnoux in France. I remember staying at a creepy old hotel, and not being able to sleep, in fear that that big bastard Nosferatu was going to join me for a late-night blood bath. It was the most depressing room I have ever been in. Must have been a morgue or something in the past. I wish they had given the room to Charlie, as he loves a good bit of Gothic Horror.

The sun in France was battering the life out of me; it was stupidly hot, but luckily these outdoor gigs had shaded areas to stand in. Moving on to pastures new, we arrived at Les Jardins, Bagnols-sur-Cèze, France. This was another hot day, but still we battled on and gave the French fans what they wanted – well, as much as we could without Mick MacNeil and Brian McGee.

Two days later, on the 18th, we were back in Germany and playing at the Motopark, Magdeburg. What a great gig this was. The stage was built at the bottom of a steep hill. We had done our soundcheck and were eating before the gig, something that had to be finished at least two hours before going onstage. This time we had another chance to have a kick about, but the ground was strangely empty. Where were the audience? Then we heard the throng of voices from the top of the hill. It was like the scene in the film *Zulu*, when the warriors come over the hill in their thousands to face the thin red line defending Rourke's Drift. There are 60,000 plus getting into place, and we're going to give them a show. The show was filmed too. One cameraman kept getting in Charlie's way, so the wee man turned on him and booted him up the arse. That's Charlie all over.

Rock Kingdom Festival, Bellinzona, Switzerland was next. I think this was the gig we did with the dearly departed legendary Irish songstress Sinead O'Connor. Clocks with wooden cuckoos, and Toblerones the size of a small mountain range, and tiny wee knives for getting stones out of horses' hooves and picking yer teeth. Marvellous. The gig was great, the people, the food, the scenery – and we weren't too shabby either.

Next we are off to the seaside at Six-Fours-les-Plages, Toulon. The gig is Festival Les Voix du Gaou, and it is scorching hot. From the stage we can see lots of expensive boats and classy hotels, shops and restaurants. There are lots of people at this one, and at the back of the stage is the Mediterranean, looking resplendent and inviting in this hotter than hell weather in July.

This was a hard gig, due to the heat. When it came to playing the set, we could all do it in our sleep. It had been a great time for me, most of it, just being out and about, with people that enjoyed the band.

* * *

20 July is Mick MacNeil's birthday. One Simple Minds fact you may not know is that the band (the original) has three Cancerians in it. Jim, Mick and myself.

The Last-Ever Gig

The next gig turns out to be the last gig I ever play with the band, unless someone can sprinkle some nostalgia dust and has the five original players to play together once more. We are all fit and able, and I can tell you that we still sound better than anyone else who has the pleasure of playing our songs.

The last-ever gig was on 21 July 1998 at a Roman amphitheatre: the Ancient Theatre of Fourvière, Lyon. We met an old friend, Henry McGrogan, who has looked after Iggy Pop for years and is, currently, managing the Corrs. The girls and their brother, Jim Corr, were playing support for us that day. They were like wee fairies, and very nice mannerly girls. We ended the tour with a powerful performance. Every man has done their duty, we get pished and we go home.

8. What Next?

I arrived home to see my lovely Wendy and my two boys, Kai and Dylan.

We moved from Pollokshields to Aberfoyle, in the Trossachs, Scotland – the Rob Roy country that the Scrabble board had foretold. I got into the local Lower Highland league football team, Aberfoyle Rob Roy.

I had my studio on the go, and worked with Graeme and Neil from Wet Wet Wet, writing for a singer I was managing at that time, Angela Capel. I also worked with Gordy Goudie with the band I was managing, Sound Buggy. All this time I was waiting for a call, to get back to work with Simple Minds. Jim Kerr called a couple of times, but nothing concrete was happening. Mel Gaynor had come up to Scotland on a visit, and we worked on stuff in the studio. We found out that Simple Minds were advertised for a gig at the SECC in Glasgow, for a charity concert for Kosovo taking place in May 1999. I called the Simple Minds office in Edinburgh and they said there was no gig. Mel and I were not convinced. When I asked who is booking the bands, I was told that it was Jim Kerr of Simple Minds. Simple Minds were going to play but Jim never called to let us know that we weren't required – and to top that, the word was put out that Mel and I weren't available for the gig! My mate, Jonathan Watson, and me decided to put together a comedy version of one of his characters with Mel and I playing with him. Phillip Differ, the comedy writer, and work partner of Jonnie, came up with lyrics for the song for us to play: P Diddy's version of the Led Zeppelin classic 'Kashmir', which P Diddy called 'Come with Me'.

We rehearsed. There was Mel on drums and myself on lead guitar, my pal Trevor Steven on guitar, Ally McCoist on bass, Phillip Differ on guitar, and Jonnie Watson on vocals as Frankie Boy. And we had four beautiful dancers from the Dennistoun Palais intertwining with us as we strutted about the stage. We passed Simple Minds, the pale version, on our way into the gig. Our dressing room was raucous, and the only one to come in was Eddie Duffy, the Number 12 bass player. The girls were singing along with the rest of us in the dressing room, songs from the Southside of Glasgow hymn book. It was off its nut. We went on, and

The charity Kosovo band Phillip Differ, Trevor Steven, Jonnie Watson, Mel Gaynor, Ally McCoist and Derek

the Simple Minds fans were baffled to see Mel and I onstage. We went down a storm, and partied on afterwards, still without seeing anyone from Simple Minds. That was how I parted company with Simple Minds again. However, I did record tracks in a studio in Glasgow for the *Black & White* album a good while after.

May the Forbes Be With You

I had been asked to do a radio interview by a man called Ethan Dettenmaier, who had a show in Los Angeles called *Combat Radio*. It was broadcast on LA Talk Radio in Hollywood. I really enjoyed our interview. Following the interview, Ethan suggested that I do my own show. At first, I wasn't that keen, which probably had something to do with confidence, then I thought, *well, why not?* The name of my show was *May the Forbes Be With You*, which had been coined by a friend's very young son. He was *Star Wars* daft and had been playing with a toy lightsaber at home, when his mother heard him say, 'May the Forbes be with you!' My co-host was Ethan Dettenmaier and the show was live on LA Talk Radio every Friday night for two years; I could do the show from wherever I was, be it in Hollywood or at home in Glasgow. I would just sit down for an hour and talk with a variety of luminaries of the film world – producers, directors, actors – as well as musicians, managers, sportspeople, and anyone else who gave up their time.

On one occasion, Combat Radio were doing a big show at the Jon Lovitz Comedy Club at Universal Studios for me. It was strange to see my name emblazoned on a fifty-foot jumbotron (a huge TV screen), at the entrance to Universal Studios. 'Combat Radio Presents … Derek Forbes at the Jon Lovitz Comedy Club'. A few days before, I received a call in the early hours of the morning. It was Jim Kerr. He had read on social media that one of the guys from the support act had said he was excited to be supporting Simple Minds at Universal City in a few days. Jim was irate. I told him to hold on; I had never used the name Simple Minds anywhere in advertising for this show. All the publicity we needed was from my own radio show, *May the Forbes Be With You*, and *Combat Radio*, which together broadcast to millions of listeners worldwide on LA Talk Radio. Jim said that he and Charlie had worked hard to keep the brand going, and they were really proud of what had been achieved over the years. … *he and Charlie achieved over the years*, I wasn't quite sure how to react to that statement. We signed off from each other with the traditional Simple Minds parting shot: 'I'd hander ye anywhere.'

Doing the radio show was a wonderful experience, but after two years, I stopped; I needed a change.

* * *

A few years ago, there was an attempt to put the original Simple Minds band together for a special recording, not an original song, but one written by some American band. A bit strange to say the least. Mick, Brian and myself said, *why not write a new track and split the writing five ways, and release that?* Jim said no, and that was when we realised that there was no chance of anything happening until our egos had dissipated. What a travesty for the fans! The most recent contact I had was to take part in a Paramount Pictures documentary about the band, but Brian, Mick and I decided against. We have other plans.

Outro: Throwing the Last Stone

I have been seeing Mick MacNeil and Brian McGee a lot recently, and our regrouping will continue with exciting things, as it says in the 'Book of Brilliant Things'. We were talking one night in Mick's house in Vatersay, just over a small bridge from the Isle of Barra. Brian and I had brought our legendary producer John Leckie with us for a few days filming and recording. Mick's brother, Donnie, looked after the studio for us, and he will eternally be named Donnie Spielberg from now on. He was great.

We all sat around the table, telling and retelling stories from our past life together. At one point Mick got a bit serious and told us that he had always felt bad about the way both Brian and I were treated, and how the band should have stood up for us at the end of our journey with them. Mick told me how he couldn't believe that they offered me, for all my years of hard work with the band, an old Volvo Estate, worth £400 at the time, and an extremely low offer from Bruce Findlay for royalties for all my songwriting with the band. Luckily, I was smart enough to refuse. I was disappointed at that nonsense even being mooted to me straight after being shown the door. So, all I got was what was due to me anyway, and not a red cent for a golden handshake. Bad form, as Captain James Hook would say.

But I must say to all the loyal fans who still follow the band, you will be in for a special treat quite soon. I hope you enjoy reading my book and hope to see you somewhere soon … Thank you, one and all.

Derek Forbes … Big Dan

Outtakes

Derek as George Harrison and Brian McGee as Terry Thomas

Jim Kerr, also undercover

On Tour with the Crew

Andy Battye: Top guitar and bass tech for Charlie and myself. We travelled on planes with the England Cricket team and Andy became famous for supplying the grass joints for Ian Botham in a hotel in New Zealand. When I asked for water instead of alcohol for the last show in Japan, Andy replaced my water with cold sake. I took a big swig of the supposed water, and nearly drowned in the familiar taste of a very strong sipping sake.

Dougie Wragg: Famous for slapping Brian after Brian gave him the Whore's Frip at the back of his legs. Also legendary for falling asleep in the PA's bass bin during a show in Bremen, at the Aladdin Club.

Big Dougie Cowan: Famous for being named the Boy with the Angel Long Hair, by Victoria, an Italian girlfriend of mine. Dougie's hair at the time was as thin as the elbow of my late granny's cardigan. A man, also known as Dougie Bugliatto, after attempting to request a receipt at a border in Italy on the Peter Gabriel Tour. Dougie is no longer with us. I drove to Bonnyrigg with Brian McGee for the big man's funeral. Jim and Charlie were there. Although a very sad day, we managed to have a laugh with stories about Big Dougie Bugliatto. We were all shocked that he had gone at so young an age (40). At the cemetery, Jim and Charlie were part of the party lowering the big man into the ground. Brian and I hummed the theme to *Star Trek*, a thing we used to do when Big Dougie entered the room. Lenny Love was at the funeral, and Johnny Ramsay. It was great to see everyone, but not great to part with Dougie fae Space. RIP.

Billy Wharton: Famous for arriving at gigs like and demanding, like some kind of cowboy, 'I want a double brandy and a coffee right now before we start.' RIP.

Roxy: Big Roxy, top man, gentle giant from Birmingham. Famous for sitting high up on the light truss and rolling joints for the band at the end of the show, pre-encore. I would look up and Roxy would drop a lit joint to me, and the band would all take a toke, before returning to the stage for an encore or three.

Bill the truck driver: Scottish Bill, famous for working with The Who and Pink Floyd, remarkable trucker.

Eddie Cairns: Spider, great roadie, driver and Lord Protector of the band. Took a joke and kept our spirits up when things went wrong.

George Golfi: Gay Greek Australian hairdresser. Absolutely hilarious. On the airplanes he would grip the arms of his seat for take-off and stretch out like he was petrified, eyes popping and white knuckles. It was only an act. George is the hands playing the drums in the 'Glittering Prize' video when I was not included.

Peter 'Samurai Sam' Kozub: Peter Kozub, famous for being the hairdresser for Princess Margaret. He also gave me a haircut just before a gig, and ran the scissors across my face accidentally. When I looked in the mirror I asked, 'What do you call that haircut … a Nikki Lauda?' Received the nickname Samurai Sam for pulling a tiny penknife out at an altercation in San Francisco. He then charmed the policewoman who led him away, calling her 'darling'. RIP.

David and Jaine Henderson: Famous for both being there in the beginning. David made the musical box intro tape and fashioned the blue head from his father's police siren and a glass head. Jaine was Jim's girlfriend and our lighting girl. They were both excellent at their jobs.

Johnny Ramsay: Big Johnny, famous for his amazing Live Sound and also for protecting me the year after a fight I had in a pub in Adelaide with a guy dressed like a skinhead. He bumped into my 65-year-old great-uncle at the bar, and I said, 'Haw, whit are you fuckin' daein?' He stared at me. I said: 'Whit are you fuckin' looking at? Are you oot for yer fuckin' Halloween?' and then punched him and knocked him to the floor. The bouncers grabbed me, him and my wee great-uncle Alex Letford. They made me shake hands with the arsehole and we both went back into the bar. Simple Minds were having a band meal. Also famous for being asked to stop smoking on a flight to Italy, but won the right to smoke where he was, so he lit up the full pack of twenty cigarettes and smoked the lot.

Frank Gallagher: Galigula, famous for a million things. Funny, tough, great sound man, eyebrow salesman. I once called his room in a New York Hotel, using an American accent. Famous for speaking to the band from the desk to the monitors whilst the gig was in full flight. To Mick he would say, 'Morag, yer too loud.' I would get 'Hun, yer oot the mix.' What a character.

Matt Dunn: Yer auld da, famous for being there always. Stealing a bike in Copenhagen, giving it to a drunken me, who got arrested for going round the Oddfellows Palace, shouting: 'Why are you not at the Falklands' to the guards. The police made me take the bike back via the boot of their car, and I had to take my laces out, with which they tied the boot shut with the bike in there. Matt was also known as Granny Finger. I'll just leave that there.

'Metal Mickey' Norrie: famous for all things merchandise. Teamed with Matt Dunn, they were a formidable pair.

Paul Kerr: Famous for being Paul Kerr, Rubber Gub, Norris the Rubber Man. Tour Manager and provider of the stage at Barrowland. Staunch ally. Middle Kerr brother.

Steve Pollard: Famous for pretending he is straight. When I told him I was getting married he asked, 'To a woman?' Big good-looking bastard from Canada. Does lights – still! Best lights for *New Gold Dream* tour, while I was there. Big Johnny crashed the truck when we were recording a TV programme in Paris. Both Johnny and Pollard were given a scare but were alright. We played in Brussels that night.

In the Van

Simple Minds had a variety of tour vans, in which we would saturate our heads with a strange mix of music. These albums and artistes would inadvertently mold our musical minds.

We would make up cassette tapes for the long journeys across the UK and Europe. Jim's forte was writing travelogues as he watched the world go by through the bus window. Not a traditional singer but more of a narrator, and part-time gymnast, onstage at least. To this day he is still bending about like a spaced yoga teacher.

On the music front we would listen to Cat Stevens – a lot – Talking Heads, Chic, the Pretenders, Magazine, Kraftwerk, Fischer Z, Ivor Cutler, Stanley Clarke and George Duke, Sly and the Family Stone, Front 242, David Bowie, Peter Gabriel, Iggy Pop, the Velvet Underground, Roxy

Music, Be-Bop Deluxe, Ultravox (pre Midge), and many more ... Eddie Cairns had the unfortunate joy of driving us all over Europe, a job that used to be Brian McGee's. We would make up tapes that would end in some harmless abuse directed at old Spider (Eddie Cairns). 'Lads, lads, who is that baldy man driving the bus? Is he a ferret or what?' Oh how we laughed as we ran at speed to get away from the raging Spider. Off we sped into the night, heading for our favourite service station; I wish we were all together again for more adventures, without a care in the world.

A Typical Tour Day

After another Saturday night – which was every night in the life of a professional rock band on tour – we would wake up, usually late and usually still a bit fragile from our exploits the evening before. Those of us who could stomach a breakfast would load up with a full English – or if we were across the pond, it would be something like French toast or pancakes with maple syrup and crispy bacon. Then the tour manager would round us up and point us in the direction of the tour bus.

Charlie Burchill getting ready for gig

Mick MacNeil, Charlie Burchill and Brian McGee, boarding another Simple Minds tour bus, Germany

When seated and off, we would sit back and watch the scenery – or, as Bruce Watson from Big Country used to say, watch World Television. It wouldn't be long before Mick MacNeil would go round the bus asking who wanted an Irish coffee. And so, we started the daily cycle of drinking till you were tired and falling asleep on the bus. Of course, the smoke of the gods was circling around in ritualistic fashion too. My old, sorely missed friend Kirsty MacColl would proclaim that we were a 'wake up, skin up family' – and by Jove we were! After maybe a few stops at a truck stop or services, we would arrive at our hotel and sleep until the soundcheck. We would head for the bar and maybe have a cheeky snifter before running through some songs, then we would start writing new material. This was our normal routine, which we would execute almost religiously. After soundcheck we would go back to the dressing room, meet Buddha 'again', then it would be time for the pre-match meal. If we were lucky, we took caterers with us. I became a vegetarian for six months in the early '80s along with others in the band, following Jim's lead. But I didn't like vegetables, so I got back on the meat. Then I tried it again and remained vegetarian for 17 years, until one night at Peter Pang's Chinese restaurant in East Kilbride, when I was conned by my pall Ally McCoist into believing that I was eating some vegetarian chicken.

My Guitars

In February 1971 I started off with a Dallas Arbiter acoustic guitar. It cost £1, and it came with a case. My mother gave me the money. I bought it from a friend, Franny Shields, in Castlemilk, Glasgow, and the first tune I learned to play was the riff from 'Badge' by Cream, followed by 'Love Like a Man' by Ten Years After. I played constantly for two weeks. I had to prise the guitar from my sore, shredded, blistered fingers and laid it down for six months.

I love acoustic guitars, of which I have many. My favourite is my Tobacco Burst Gibson J-45 Custom. It is ideal for all sorts of playing and it inspires me. On the bass guitar side, my favourite at the moment is my White Fender Precision Custom USA, for live work.

My 1978 Fender Precision Fretless USA, natural finish and gold scratchplate, is fantastic for my fretless songs. I have two 1978 Fender Precision USA fretted basses. One is my original Sienna Sunburst (red and yellow), the other is the exact same year, colour and model. I played Wal and Vigier and they are top-quality guitars, but you cannot get any cooler than strutting around the stage with a Fender Precision strapped to your back.

My favourite electric guitars: Gibson Les Paul. Fender Telecaster. Gibson SG. Gibson ES-335. Fender Stratocaster. Danelectro DC59.

Other Bands I have played in

FourGoodMen – Mick MacNeil, Bruce Watson, Ian Donaldson, Jane Button, Kenny Hyslop, Steve Fox Harris, Jim Prime, Malky Button, Kirk Brandon, Phil Kane, Carrie MacNeil, Vonnie McHugh, Frank O'Hare, Alex MacNeil.

James 'Iggy Pop' Osterburg – without whom my career in music may never have happened.

Ex Simple Minds (XSM) – Brian McGee, Owen Paul McGee, Andy Gall, Derek Forbes.

Kirk Brandon's 10:51 – John McNutt, Art Smith, Derek Forbes.

FourGoodMen, Ian Donaldson, Mick MacNeil and Derek, Boston, USA

10:51 Tour, Dresden, 1994

Outtakes

Ken Lloyd and Derek recording for an Oblivion Dust album, Los Angeles

Oblivion Dust – Taka Motamura, Ken Shibuya, Kazu. Songs written by Forbes and Ray McVeigh.

Spear of Destiny – Kirk Brandon, Derek Forbes, Chris Bell, Woz, Steve Fox Harris.

Big Country – first with Mike Peters and later with Simon Hough. Bruce Watson, Jamie Watson and Mark Brzezicki were always in the band.

The Alarm – Mike Peters, Steve Grantley, James Stephenson, Derek Forbes.

Los Mondo Bongo – Mike Peters, Derek Forbes, Steve Fox Harris, Pablo Cook.

Derek Forbes Band – John McNutt, Marc Iezzi, Tim McKinstrie, Danny Beissel.

May the Forbes be with You on LA Talk Radio – John McNutt, Art Smith, George Porter, Breezelle Fox, Saia Lundy, Guylaine Vivarat.

And if you want to see me with my band, look for:

Derek Forbes & the Dark. Derek Forbes, Toni Soave, Brian McNeill, James Brecko.

Not Forgetting

Simple Minds friends who have passed on:

Tony Donald, original bass player

Billy Wharton, Sound Engineer

Dougie Wragg, Road Crew

Dougie Cowan, Road Crew and Boffin

Peter Kozub, Hair, Make-up and Wardrobe

Rab Clark, Merchandise

Eddie Cairns, Driver and Road Crew

Absent Friends

Walter Smith. Craig Brown. Andy Goram, The Matriarch.

Words from Jon Carin

My introduction to Derek Forbes happened to a 15-year-old me. 1980.
Schoolmates sat me down and said, 'Listen to this!'
'Thirty Frames a Second' blasted my hair back.
Then, they said, 'Wait for it!'
'Twist/Run/Repulsion.'
'Today I Died Again.'
'This Fear of Gods.'
'Now you're ready,' they said.
'I Travel.'
'These are all fucking bass lines!' I exclaimed.
'Yup', they replied.
'This guy's a monster.'
'He is indeed.'
'So the songs are all written over his amazing bass riffs.'
'Yup'.
I couldn't get his riffs out of my head.
Next year, 'In Trance as Mission', 'Sweat in Bullet', 'Love Song', 'The American' … bass lines!
And again the next year, 'Glittering Prize', 'Promised You a Miracle', 'Big Sleep' and the mother lode: 'New Gold Dream'.
Who plays like that and gets away with it?
And the next year, 'Waterfront', 'Up on the Catwalk', 'Speed Your Love to Me'.
Those songs based on the mighty and hypnotic bass lines of Derek Forbes are still some of my favorite music ever made.
He's the bassist in my dream band.
Anytime you're ready, Derek. X

Jon Carin, musician, producer, songwriter, Pink Floyd, Roger Waters, The Who, David Gilmour

Words from Michael Mertens

I don't recall the first time I met Derek; I think it must have been in the rehearsal studio when Propaganda was preparing for the live shows in London at the Ambassador Theatre in 1984. Wherever it was, we hit it off right from the start. Derek had a kind of legendary status as an ex-member of Simple Minds. At that time, Propaganda was just a sidekick for me; my main job was percussionist at the Duesseldorf Symphony Orchestra, where we performed classical opera at the Duesseldorf Opera House.

My English language was basic and there were quite a few moments where I felt rather insecure, but with Derek, that was never a problem. He has a lot of humour and was always a very friendly companion. I guess the mutual respect and appreciation for the musicianship of each other made that happen.

Propaganda played over forty concerts all over Europe, some shows in Japan and six or seven shows on the East Coast of the United States of America.

Derek remains a friend up to this day and has given me wonderful memories. He invited us all to his house in the Scottish countryside many times to write new songs. I happily stayed there for six months and had a wonderful time. I will never forget taking a ride on Derek's horse, Blue, through the Scottish countryside. What an amazing time we had; I will never forget.

Michael Mertens, musician, Propaganda

Words from Greta Brinkman

1981. Bass players all over the globe (OK, maybe just me) pricked up their ears at the amazing double album *Sons and Fascination/Sister Feelings Call* from Scottish band Simple Minds. *Sister Feelings Call* featured not just the epic 'Theme for Great Cities' but also the timeless classic, 'The American'. A fledgling bassist in my first punk band. I heard both songs on local US college radio while washing dishes in a restaurant and became a fan immediately.

Why was this record so special? The bass playing. There was a lot of great music that year, but Derek Forbes' masterful blend of slappita-poppita and solid, thoughtful rock bass immediately elevated this album well above the herd. I listened to this record literally hundreds of times. I still listen to it today! Years later, Facebook was a thing. Delighted to be added to his friends list, I learned that Derek was not only still playing but also had a witty way of writing with a healthy amount of snark towards ex-bandmates. What musician cannot relate to that

I read and enjoy every rock autobio I can find, and I'm really, really looking forward to this.

Greta Brinkman, bassist, Moby, Debbie Harry, White Cross, Jayne County, Pigface

Derek Forbes

Words from Gavin Mitchell

As long as I can remember I've been surrounded and influenced by and loved music: my elder brother introduced me to an eclectic mix of the Beatles, the Stones, the Groundhogs, Argent, Free, Emerson, Lake & Palmer, Tangerine Dream, the Nice, Roxy Music, Bowie, King Crimson, Stevie Wonder, Diana Ross, Issac Hayes. Theme tunes like *Fireball XL5* and *The Persuaders!* Soundtracks like *Saturday Night Fever* and *One from the Heart*, electronica, punk, new wave, Beethoven … you name it! But when you're old enough to discover your own band, your own sound, your own voice and tribe … well that's a whole new development entirely, a rite of passage, a coming of age!

As Bowie said, 'Tomorrow belongs to those that can hear it coming.' The first time I heard Simple Minds, that momentous day had arrived! They sounded like nothing I'd ever heard before, familiar and yet alien, and they were from Glasgow; my hometown, but with European aspirations and sensibilities! They had style, lyrics that were mysterious, ambiguous, and an ambitious original sound. That unique sound was in no small part down to this man! He was originally a guitarist, but no one plays the bass or creates riffs like him and, for my money, with Brian McGee and later Mel Gaynor, he was the engine room, the pulse, heartbeat and behemoth of the band. 'Sweat in Bullet', 'The American', 'Thirty Frames a Second' – for which I passed my Higher in art designing a cover – and of course 'I Travel', to name but a few. I saw the Minds many times, but I remember 21 December 1983, with great fondness: the reopening of the greatest venue in the world, the mighty Glasgow Barrowland ballroom. The atmosphere was electric, expectations high and sweaty bodies at maximum capacity. Out of the darkness, the first note to be heard in the newly opened venue broke the air … not just a bassline, it was a pulse, a throb of strength and power, a clarion call to all and an unofficial anthem to our great city, the iconic 'Waterfront'. We all roared and went wild, unified as one!

Little did I know, years later while making a short film, the make-up girl would say to me: 'I hear you're a Simple Minds fan and you do impressions of the band?' *Yeah*, I said tentatively. I then demonstrated some of Jim Kerr's early moves: the change the light bulb; the clap the dug; and the 'butter a piece' as I called them. 'Can you do the bass player?' she asked. *Big Derek Forbes? My favourite. Yeah. He has two basic moves.*

He moves from leg to leg like this. And he bounces like this. She started to laugh, 'That's brilliant. You got him spot on!' *Oh, are you a fan?* I asked. 'No, he's, my husband.' I was mortified! I wanted the ground to open and swallow me!

A few weeks later, I was invited over for dinner. I was excited but jumpy. 'Are you nervous?' she asked while driving me over to their home. *Aye Wendy. You don't understand, I used tae have posters of your husband on my wall!* It was fine. Derek was utterly charming, and we got on like a house on fire. Since then I've had the honour and pleasure of seeing and hearing him in many guises, whether it be with Propaganda or Big Country, backing singing for Iggy Pop, working with Kirk Brandon, reimagining his own early work, his present band Derek Forbes and the Dark – or even playing 'Ziggy Stardust' in the kitchen, on a guitar once owned by Tony McPhee from the mighty Groundhogs, the way that Mick Ronson showed him, no less. He is never less than brilliant! In my opinion, the greatest bass player Scotland ever produced. All of which I'm proud to say was richly recognised when he received his Ivor Novello, not to mention his induction into the Barrowland Hall of Fame with aforementioned luminaries such as Mr Bowie and Mr Pop. A lot of people say you should never meet your heroes. Well, I'm incredibly lucky: not only have I, but I'm proud to call him a dear, dear friend.

Love on ya, Captain!

Gavin Mitchell, actor

Acknowledgements

Mick MacNeil and Brian McGee for unrepeatable stories and laughter. John Leckie for inspiration and encouragement.

Thanks to Pete Walsh for being my co-pilot on all our journeys north.

Eddie Cairns, for keeping me right. John McNutt, Marc Iezzi, Danny Beissel and Tim McKinstrey for showing me Philadelphia and all its Jawn. Yo Cuz!

My sons Kai and Dylan, and grandson Layne for carrying the torch … I thank you.